Introduction

Back when Kentucky's bluegrass region was a wild and empty corner of a primitive British colony, learned European composers like Mozart and Beethoven were writing sophisticated pieces for the mandolin. In the late 1800's a mandolin craze swept America and parts of Europe; countless mandolin orchestras were organized involving both amateurs and professional musicians.

In the view of history 1939 was only last week. Yet in October of that year when Bill Monroe and his Blue Grass Boys first swept onto Nashville's Grand Ole Opry stage, the audience exploded as though no one had ever heard a mandolin before. And they hadn't—not bluegrass mandolin. It was a brand new and compelling sound.

Since then bluegrass has opened up new vistas for that formerly delicate and fragile-sounding instrument. The bluegrass mandolin can moan on a gutsy blues or it can roar over a fast-paced breakdown. It can still play a sweet tremolo or it can produce a sparkling cascade of notes like a three-finger banjo roll.

By the early 1970's the mandolin had begun to filter into the pop music field, and it was successfully employed on quite a few hit records. A large audience outside the bluegrass world was introduced to the mandolin for the first time and liked it. None of the numerous pop performers to use it, however, came up with new ideas comparable to the innovations of bluegrass mandolinists.

As you will learn in the course of this book, bluegrass mandolin is a varied musical landscape. Exploring it can be a fascinating and exciting experience. But it is also an area where fresh ideas and new twists to old ones are out there in the wilderness, waiting for us to find them.

The basics

Parts of the mandolin

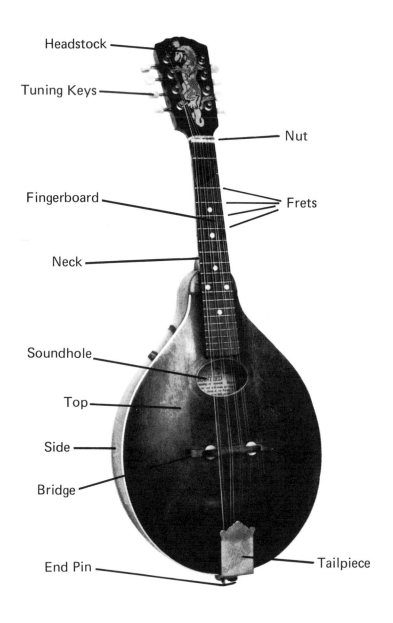

Headstock

Tuning Keys

Nut

Fingerboard

Frets

Neck

Soundhole

Top

Side

Bridge

End Pin

Tailpiece

Bluegrass Mandolin

by Jack Tottle

Oak Publications

New York · London · Sydney

About The Author

Jack Tottle is a professional musician with long experience
in a variety of musical styles and in teaching. He is a member of
the bluegrass group *Tasty Licks*. Among the recordings on
which his playing is heard are *Tasty Licks*. (Rounder 0106)
and his solo album *Back Road* (Rounder 0067).

Acknowledgements

A number of people contributed importantly to this book.
I would like to thank Fred Bartenstein, Joe Hickerson,
Alan Jabbour, Peter Kuykendall, Joshua Lewin, Dan Marcus,
the Rounder Collective, Brian Sinclair, Rose Zak, and,
especially, Alex.

Photographs

E. B. Boatner	5, 18, 55, 75, 87, 117, 126, 159 (bottom right, bottom left, top left)
Ron Elsis	82 (left)
Hank Holland	134
Don Kissil	141, 143, 158
Ernie Koerlin	109
Kim Ladewig	Cover, 89 (top left)
Jim McGuire	82 (right)
David Weintraub	73
Alan Whitman	13, 25
Herbert Wise	158 (left), 159 (top right)
Unknown	89 (bottom)
courtesy of *Muleskinner News*	89 (top right), 111, 149 (bottom)
courtesy of *RCA Records*	149 (top)

Book design by Iris Weinstein and Mark Stein

Copyright © 1975 by Oak Publications,
A Division of Embassy Music Corporation, New York, NY.

US International Standard Book Number: 0.8256.0154.1
UK International Standard Book Number: 0.7119.0320.4
Library of Congress Catalog Card Number: 74-77692

Exclusive Distributors:
Music Sales Corporation
257 Park Avenue South, New York, NY 10010 USA
Music Sales Limited
8/9 Frith Street, London W1V 5TZ England
Music Sales Pty. Limited
120 Rothschild Street, Rosebery, Sydney, NSW 2018, Australia

Printed in the United States of America by
Victor Graphics

Contents

(cont'd)

Tuning

To start off, you'll want to be sure your mandolin is in tune. Your neighborhood music store can easily tune it for you—which they should do free of charge—but you will, of course, want to be able to tune it yourself.

Tuning is done by tightening or loosening the strings by means of the tuning keys. Tuning each string properly depends on hearing when the string you are tuning is equal in pitch to a note from another source which is used for reference.

The mandolin's eight strings are tuned in pairs. As the strings of each pair are tuned identically, each pair is referred to as one string. The strings are designated as follows:

1st or E string
2nd or A string
3rd or D string
4th or G string

Tuning from a piano. Any instrument can be tuned from any other, once you know where the corresponding notes fall. Notes on the piano equivalent to open strings on the mandolin are shown below. (Before tuning from another instrument, you naturally want to be sure that the instrument you are using for reference is itself in tune.)

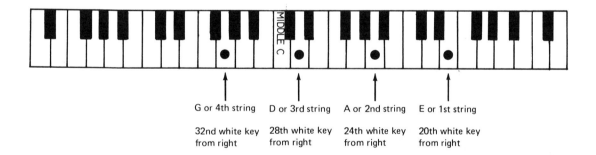

G or 4th string	D or 3rd string	A or 2nd string	E or 1st string
32nd white key from right	28th white key from right	24th white key from right	20th white key from right

The pitch pipe. Music stores sell an item called a pitch pipe. There are different models for different instruments. The pitch pipe used for the mandolin is the same as for the violin, since the two instruments are tuned the same way. It consists of four pipes mounted together. Blowing on the various pipes produces the four different notes to which the mandolin's strings are tuned.

Pitch pipes are, unfortunately, not absolutely precise. The pitch of the note produced can vary with how hard you blow into it, and it tends to become increasingly inaccurate with prolonged use.

The tuning fork. The most precise and easily portable reference for tuning is the tuning fork. A small and inexpensive tuning fork corresponding to the 2nd or A string of the mandolin can be purchased through any music store. (It is called the A or 440 tuning fork because it vibrates at the rate of 440 cycles per second.) Once the 2nd string is tuned to it, the other strings are tuned from the second string, as described in the section following this one.

Set the tuning fork vibrating by tapping one of the prongs against a firm, but not rigid, surface. The heel of your shoe will do fine. (If you hit it against a hard surface like wood or metal you may dent it slightly and throw it off pitch.)

While it is vibrating, place the handle securely against the bridge of your mandolin and you will hear the note clearly as the mandolin begins to vibrate in the same frequency. Tune the second string to correspond with this note.

Tuning the mandolin to itself. If you have tuned the second string to a tuning fork as described above, or if the mandolin has gotten partially out of tune after being tuned by any other method, it can be put in tune as follows.

Each open string is tuned to the same note as the next *lower* (in pitch) string when noted at the 7th fret. Therefore:

>1st string open=2nd string, 7th fret
>2nd string open=3rd string, 7th fret
>3rd string open=4th string, 7th fret

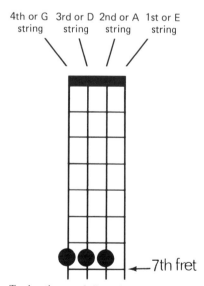

Tuning the mandolin to itself. The heavy dots on the fingerboard diagram are to indicate that any string played open should produce the same note as the next lower (in pitch) string played at the 7th fret.

Thus if your second string is tuned to the tuning fork, you can play it at the 7th fret to get the right note for the first string. Then play the 3rd string at the 7th fret and tune that string until it corresponds with the 2nd string open. The fourth string is similarly tuned to the third.

Holding the mandolin

Always use a strap. If you get in the habit of playing while resting the instrument on your lap, you will find it awkward to stand and play (which is how most playing is done).

A narrow piece of leather makes a good strap. A shoulder pad for added comfort can be made from a wider piece if desired. The strap can be looped around the narrow part of the headstock next to the nut (under the strings) and attached to the end pin. If your mandolin has a scroll, you can attach the strap to the scroll itself instead of the headstock.

The length of the strap is such that the lower portion of the mandolin comes slightly above the waist. Use of the strap in this manner will support the mandolin fully, leaving the left hand free to move up and down the fingerboard. It also keeps the mandolin roughly parallel with your body, which is important to effective and comfortable positioning of the left hand.

The pick

The pick should be fairly stiff. It should not be totally rigid, but it can be almost so.

There is a temptation to start out using a highly flexible pick because it's so easy to play up and down across the strings, Unfortunately, this tends to produce a flabby tone, snappy pick noise, and may limit volume.

Some of the more common pick shapes are shown below:

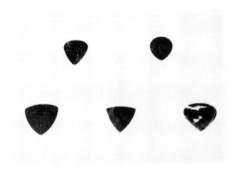

Rounded and pointed picks produce different tones, and their use varies with individual preference.

Picks are made from plastic and also from tortoise shell. Many players prefer the tone produced by tortoise shell, though it is more expensive and more difficult to find. (Some plastic picks are made to look like tortoise shell, so be careful that a salesman doesn't give you the wrong kind. Real tortoise shell is harder and shinier than plastic.)

The right hand: basic picking

Watching a capable performer, it is easy to get the idea that everything depends on the dexterity of the left hand as its fingers move rapidly over the fingerboard. While it is true that the left hand must be well controlled and coordinated, it is absolutely impossible to play good music without full command over tone, dynamics, smoothness and rhythm. Each of these aspects depends on the right hand. It is thus quite important that you achieve, at the outset, a loose, comfortable and controlled action of picking the strings.

First, look at the pictures below to see how the pick is held. Try holding your pick the same way.

 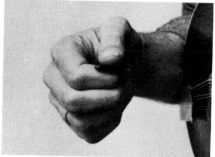

Next, strike your 4th string downward with the pick. The motion should come from your wrist, not your arm. Hit the string several times more in an even rhythm and listen carefully to the result. Try varying your hand position slightly to get both a comfortable position and a firm, confident sound from the string. Then try playing each of the other strings, individually, in the same manner.

See how loosely you can hold the pick when you hit the strings. Until you have grown into a comfortable, easy right hand picking motion, don't try to play hard or loud as this is likely to cause your hand to tense and your sound to be choppy. Right now smoothness is far more important than volume.

Appendix IV at the back of the book gives a still more detailed description of the right hand. After you have worked with the pick on your own for a while you may want to check it for additional ideas.

The left hand

The job of the left hand is to shorten that portion of the string that will vibrate when the pick strikes it. The shorter the vibrating portion of the string, the higher the pitch of the note produced.

Support the mandolin gently with your left hand, letting the neck rest at the base of the index or first finger, as shown in the picture. Notice that the thumb rests above the neck, and that there is an open space between the thumb and the hand. The neck is not pushed all the way back to the place where the thumb joins the hand.

To sound a note higher than any string's fundamental (open) note, a finger of the left hand presses the string against the fingerboard just behind one of the frets. Thus instead of vibrating all the way from the bridge to the nut when struck, the string vibrates only from the bridge to that particular fret.

With the third (or ring) finger of your left hand, press the 2nd (or A) string behind the fifth fret. Remember that you want the string to press firmly *against* the fifth fret. If your finger is too far forward "up" the neck (that is, toward the bridge) you will muffle the note. If the finger is not close enough to the fret, it may not hold the string down tightly enough, and the note may buzz.

The string is pressed down against the fingerboard by the very tip of your finger. The finger should be arched, and none of the joints should lock (or straighten out). The finger should come down on the string at an angle close to perpendicular with the fingerboard. This means that the force you apply will be straight down, rather than at an angle, and thus gives you the maximum result for your effort. It also helps keep your finger from interfering with an adjacent string by mistake. These points are generally true for any finger used on any fret. Later, when you have to move quickly from one note to another, you'll appreciate them more fully.

If the fingernails of your left hand are long, they are probably interfering with holding down the string. Cut them if necessary.

While holding the 2nd string at the fifth fret as indicated above, strike it with a firm downstroke of the pick. If the note sounds clear, fine. If not, recheck each of the instructions concerning the left hand. Sometimes altering the angle of your left wrist to your forearm will help your fingers land more squarely on the fingerboard. (Should you have reason to feel that the strings may be either too high or too low, have them checked by a qualified instrument repairman.)

If you find that pressing the strings down is hard work at first, don't worry. Your hand will gain strength as you play. The ends of your fingers may also become tender, but they will soon develop protective calluses. (Soaking, especially in hot water, impedes the formation of calluses, so try to hold this to a minimum. This doesn't mean you must stop bathing or washing dishes, but just don't soak your left hand more than necessary.)

After playing the note clearly as described above, try other notes on each of the strings. The general rule on which finger to use at any given fret (regardless of what string you are playing) is as follows:

> 1st or 2nd fret—First (or index) finger
> 3rd or 4th fret—Second (or middle) finger
> 5th or 6th fret—Third (or ring) finger
> 7th fret—Fourth (or little) finger

As you experiment, hold the string as tightly as necessary to produce a strong, clear note, *but no tighter.* Holding too tightly wastes energy, slows you down, tires you out and can produce painful cramps in your hand.

Picking single strings

The downstroke

Playing the downstroke is quite simple once you have your right hand in the correct position as described in earlier sections. Start out by hitting the fourth string open with the pick in a firm downward motion. The movement should be sharp enough so that both strings of the pair sound simultaneously and are heard as a single note.

As in all aspects of playing, the best method is the method which does not entail unnecessary motion or energy. Start your stroke near the string (perhaps ½ inch or more away). The follow-through of your stroke should take you a similar distance past the 4th string. It should not carry the pick past the next string, (in this case, the 3rd string), nor should the pick hit against this next string.

Now try each of the other open strings. Once you feel comfortable with these, try the same thing while noting the strings at various frets as described in the section on the left hand.

The down-up stroke

A great deal of mandolin playing is based on this stroke, so it is important to learn to do it well from the beginning. It consists of the downstroke, described above, followed by an upstroke which returns the pick to its original position, ready for the next downstroke.

As with the simple downstroke, make sure that both strings of the pair sound together, as a single note, on the upstroke as well as on the down. The upstroke should sound as nearly like the downstroke as possible. Achieving this depends largely on the looseness with which the pick is held.

Play a series of down-up strokes on the 4th string. As you do so count aloud:

"One, and, two, and, three, and, four, and,"

Repeat the count up to four over and over again. It should be rock steady with each beat exactly the same as the previous one. Keep it comfortably slow and very even.

The pick should be doing a downstroke each time you say "one" or "two" or "three", etc. It should be doing an upstroke each time you say the word "and" The result is a very even "down-up-down-up-down-up-down-up" with the pick.

Now do the same on each of the other open strings. Try the same idea while noting the strings at different frets as you did with the downstroke.

The slide

The slide, in its most basic form, produces the sound of two notes while the pick strikes the strings just once. For example: Place the second finger of the left hand at the third fret of the 3rd string. Play a single downstroke on the 3rd string and immediately (just as the pick finishes hitting the string) slide second finger of your left hand up to the fourth fret of the same string. As your finger slides quickly over the third fret (while continuing to press the string down) and comes to rest behind the fourth fret, a second, higher pitched, note will be produced.

Try this several times until it becomes easy, making sure that you are clearly hearing two notes in rapid succession, but are hitting the string with the pick just once.

Hammering-on

Hammering-on also produces the sound of two different notes with just a single stroke of the pick.

Hold your 3rd string down at the 2nd fret with your first finger. Play this note as a downstroke and in the next instant bring your second finger down sharply and hard at the 4th fret of the same string, producing a new, higher note. (Don't move your first finger as you do so.) As with the slide, practice until you can get two clean notes with a single pick stroke.

You can also hammer-on starting with an open string. For example, try hitting your third string open and hammering-on at the 2nd fret.

Introduction to the tremolo

If you have listened to many records of mandolin playing (as you will need to do if you expect to play the instrument yourself) or have seen it played live, you have probably heard the tremolo. It is a series of down-up strokes played so rapidly that the effect is similar to a single sustained note, such as you might hear on a fiddle, organ or electric guitar.

A later section treats the tremolo in detail. You can, however, do some useful preparation in advance by periodically spending a little time upgrading your down-up stroke.

Once you have learned to do the down-up stroke smoothly and evenly at a slow speed, try playing it just a little faster. If it starts sounding choppy or uneven, decrease the speed to the point where you have good control. Increasing your speed little by little and over a period of time, without sacrificing smoothness, will put you in good shape for the tremolo chapter.

For now, don't make a major project of it. Just work a little on it every now and then as you go along.

Bill Monroe and Curley Sechler. Known primarily as a singer, Curley also played mandolin on many of Flatt and Scruggs' classic recordings.

Keeping time and reading tablature

There is absolutely no need to read music in order to play bluegrass; none of the style's originators did. Although standard music notation is included in this book for those who wish to use it, all you will need to know is (1) how to keep time and (2) how to use a simplified notation system called *tablature*. This chapter will explain both.

Keeping time

Many of us are drawn to music because of melodies we find compelling or note sequences that excite us. Any top professional will tell you, that excellent timing is the basic requirement for playing good music. You can play the prettiest or the fanciest melodic line in the world, but if your timing is uneven, the line will sound weak.

To get a feel for keeping time, let's start off with an old warhorse everyone knows. Sing (or hum) the chorus aloud—not too fast—and tap your foot along with it. Be sure your tapping is completely even and steady. Try tapping each time you see a heavy slash mark (/):

/	/	/	/	/	/	/	/	
Oh	Sus-	an- na		Don't you	cry	for	me	I

/	/	/	/	/	/	/	/
Come from	Al- a-	bam- a	with a	Ban- jo	on	my	knee

The tapping (or beat) should be as steady as the swing of the pendulum in a grandfather clock. This is important not only for those beats which fall directly on the words of the song, but also for those beats where no syllable is sung. (See slashes after "an-na", "me" and "knee".)

These beats (indicated by the heavy slash mark) are called accented beats or on-beats.

Next, let's try tapping an offbeat after each onbeat. This means tapping exactly twice as fast, while singing at the same tempo you did before. The offbeats are indicated below by light slash marks (/). Your foot will tap on the floor once for each / and once again for each /.

Count:

1	2	3	4	1	2	3	4	1	2	3	4	1	2	3	4
/	/	/	/	/	/	/	/	/	/	/	/	/	/	/	/
Oh		Sus-		an-	na			Don't	you	cry	for	me			I

1	2	3	4	1	2	3	4	1	2	3	4	1	2	3	4
/	/	/	/	/	/	/	/	/	/	/	/	/	/	/	/
Come	from	Al-	a-	bam-	a	with	a	Ban-	jo	on	my	knee			

Make each note you sing in the chorus last just one beat—that is, just one tap of your foot. Each of these notes is called a *quarter note*.

Now, let's make sure you are really tapping *all* the beats in *Oh Susanna,* including those beats without syllables. Sing the word "rest" each time you have a beat which doesn't coincide with a syllable of the song. If you do it correctly, it will sound like this:

Oh	(rest)	Sus-	(rest)	an-	na	(rest)	(rest)	Don't you	cry	for	me	(rest)	(rest)	I
Come from	Al-	a-		bam-	a	with	a	Ban- jo	on	my	knee	(rest)	(rest)	(rest)

Counting eighth notes

One more simple step is required to relate counting to the down-up stroke you have learned with the pick. Tap out *Oh Susanna* once more, exactly as in the previous example, but think of one additional beat after each of the beats you counted before. Instead of counting "1, 2, 3, 4," as in the earlier example, you will count "1 & 2 & 3 & 4 &" as shown below:

Count:

1 & 2 & 3 & 4 &	1 & 2 & 3 & 4 &	1 & 2 & 3 & 4 &	1 & 2 & 3 & 4 &
/ / / /	/ / / /	/ / / /	/ / / /
Oh Sus-	an- na	Don't you cry for	me I
1 & 2 & 3 & 4 &	1 & 2 & 3 & 4 &	1 & 2 & 3 & 4 &	1 & 2 & 3 & 4 &
/ / / /	/ / / /	/ / / /	/ / / /
Come from Al- a-	bam- a with a	Ban- jo on my	knee

Your foot taps down against the floor on each count of "1", "2", "3", or "4" as it did previously. This time you are also counting "&" each time your foot moves back up.

Feeling comfortable with this count is important because it corresponds exactly to the usual manner of playing down-up strokes with the pick. Each count of "1", "2", "3", or "4" corresponds with a downstroke and each "&" corresponds with an upstroke. *Thus, as your foot moves downward, so will your pick. As your foot moves back up, your pick will do the same.* Notes played in this manner are called *eighth notes*.

The same count works for most country or bluegrass songs, but don't try it yet on any really fast ones. (Songs in waltz time are counted in series of three instead of four, but we'll come to that later.) You will find that counting and tapping on the above song and on additional ones you may know or have on record will greatly help your sense of rhythm and timing. It will also help you *feel* music, rather than depend on logic and memorization to understand the way musical phrases and tunes are put together.

Reading tablature

The staff The tablature staff consists of four horizontal lines. Each line represents a string of the mandolin, as indicated below:

The measure For ease of reading, vertical lines are used to divide the tablature staff into sections. Each of these sections is called a measure. The example above shows a line of tablature divided into four measures.

Time signature In most of the tunes we'll be doing, as in the songs you've already practiced counting, there will be four beats to the measure, each of these beats will be called a quarter note. This is indicated by the time signature 4/4. (Later on we'll come to tunes in waltz time with three beats to the measure. These will have the time signature 3/4.)

Notes A number written on the staff shows at which fret a given string is to be noted. The 3rd string played at the 2nd fret would be indicated:

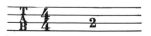

The 2nd string played open would be:

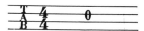

Note values 1. The quarter note. As you know from the section on counting, if you play each beat of a tune in 4/4 time (that is, both onbeat and offbeat) you are playing quarter notes. A plain stem is used to indicate that a note is played as a quarter note:

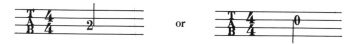

(Whether the stem points up or down does not affect how the note is played.)

As mentioned earlier, a 4/4 measure consists of four beats. Thus, if a measure is composed of quarter notes only, there will be four quarter notes to the measure. For example:

Count: 1   2   3   4

2. Eighth notes. The counting section explains that adding an additional count after each beat in a tune results in a succession of eighth notes. An individual eighth note has a stem with a flag:

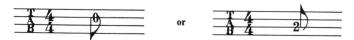

(Again, it doesn't matter which way the stem points.)

Two or more eighth notes are connected as shown below:

A measure containing only eighth notes will still have four beats. It will, however, have eight eighth notes:

Count: 1 & 2 & 3 & 4 &

Rests These indicate pauses where no note is played. An example is the earlier exercise in counting "Oh Susanna" in which you said the word "rest" on each beat where no word of the song fell.

1. Quarter rest. This is a pause of the same duration as a quarter note. It is written:

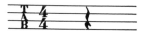

2. Eighth rest. This is a pause of the same duration as an eighth note. It is written:

Slide The symbol ⑤ indicates a slide. Unless otherwise indicated, start the slide one fret below the note given and slide up to that note. A quick slide from the 3rd to the 4th fret of the 3rd string would be written:

In the above example the final note falls squarely on the beat, with the previous note heard just an instant before. Sometimes, however, a slide is slow enough so that each note is heard on a separate beat. This is shown as:

The string is still hit only once, but the two notes are heard to fall distinctly on two beats, just as though both had been picked.

Hammering-on The symbol ⓗ means a note is to be hammered. Normally you will hammer from the fret previously noted on that string:

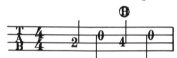

In the example above, with your finger still on the 3rd string 2nd fret, you would hammer-on at the 4th fret.

Fingering A number in parentheses above the tablature staff indicates which finger is used to play a given note. In the phrase below, for example, the second finger plays the 1st string, 5th fret. The first finger plays the 2nd string, 4th fret.

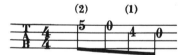

Pick direction The symbol ⊓ indicates a downstroke of the pick. An upstroke is written **V**.

Repeat sign A phrase which is to be repeated begins with the symbol ▐▐▬ and ends with ▬▐▐ . It may be a short phrase, or more often in this book, an entire verse or chorus of a song. If there is no ▐▐▬ prior to the final repeat sign, return to the beginning of the piece.

First and second endings A repeated phrase may sometimes end differently the second time than it did the first time. When this happens, the first and second endings are shown, respectively, as follows:

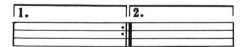

For example, the phrase:

would actually be played:

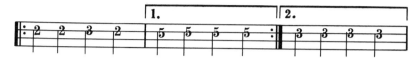

Brush stroke A sharp downward stroke across all four strings used with chords in accompaniment is indicated by a long slash mark: /

Tremolo ♩ indicates that a tremolo is played for the value of the note shown.

Doyle Lawson, a mainstay of the Country Gentleman.

Andy Statman of Country Cooking, Breakfast Special and David Bromberg's group.

Breaking the ice

A mixed bag of introductory tunes

Now to play some music! As you try out the following tunes, work on an even, flowing sound. Don't try to play fast or loud, there will be plenty of opportunity for that later.

Woody Guthrie is best known as a songwriter/singer and inspiration to countless folk-singers. As it happens, he also played the mandolin. We'll start off with a slightly simplified version of a tune he wrote. It is based on one simple repeating phrase:

Try playing it, while tapping your foot. As the phrase consists of eight eighth notes, you will play a note for each downward and each upward motion of your foot.

Notice that the *down-up-down-up* pick movement is used throughout the phrase except on the second note. The upstroke is omitted on this note, because the note is sounded by sliding from the previous one. (Take care to begin again after the slide with a down-stroke.)

After you can play the basic phrase as written above, try the same pattern moved over so that it begins on the 4th string:

The identical phrase is also played beginning on the 2nd string:

Count: 1 & 2 & 3 & 4 &

To play the tune, you need only one more phrase. This one starts like the basic phrase, but it changes after the beginning notes. Notice that you play a downstroke on the 2nd string, 5th fret followed by an upstroke on the 2nd string open, with no pause in between.

Count: 1 & 2 & 3 & 4 & 1 & 2 & 3 & 4 &

Don't forget that each time you play a quarter note, you pause for the "&" count before hitting the next note.

Once you are in good control of each of the phrases, go on to the tune itself. You will find that—throughout most of the tune—the basic phrase is played twice, then shifted to another string and played twice in the new location, then shifted again etc.

Notice that all the quarter notes are played as downstrokes, and that all series of eighth notes (except where broken by slides) are played as down-up strokes. This pattern will hold true for nearly all the playing you do, and it is quite important to adhere to it, unless otherwise indicated.

One last point: Be sure your left hand fingering is correct according to the rules given on page 11. You should be using your 2nd (middle) finger each time you play the 3rd or 4th fret and your 3rd (ring) finger at the 5th fret.

Woody's Rag, Part I

Woody Guthrie

Whenever you learn a tune, start out slow. After you can play the entire piece at a slow, steady tempo, try it a little faster, but don't lose control. You should *never* pace a tune faster than you can do the most difficult section. (In other words, guard against temptation to play the easy sections fast and then to slow down on the hard ones.)

Now, let's try a second section of *Woody's Rag.* This contains some variations of the ideas in Part I. The first phrase on which Part II is based is the following:

The other central phrase is an elaboration of the previous one. Note that there are several instances where you play a different note on an upstroke from the preceding downstroke:

As with the basic phrase of Part I, these patterns are moved across the fingerboard in the course of the tune. Notice that the last line of Part II is identical to that of Part I. (The down and upstroke symbols are omitted throughout Part II where the pick direction is obvious.)

Woody's Rag, Part II

Woody Guthrie

Wildwood Flower

This is an old favorite guitar piece. It makes a nice tune on the mandolin.

Only one phrase requires playing a given note on the downstroke, followed by a different note on the upstroke:

Play this phrase a few times by itself first; then try the whole tune. Notice that measures 7, 8, 9 and 10 are an exact repetition of measures 2, 3, 4 and 5.

The symbols above the first line of the tune are a reminder that each quarter note is played on a downstroke and each group of eighth notes is played using down-up strokes.

Red Rector with Tater Tate. Red has recorded with numerous important artists including Charlie Monroe, Hylo Brown, Walt Hensley and Don Reno and Red Smiley. He is currently performing on his own.

Oh Susanna

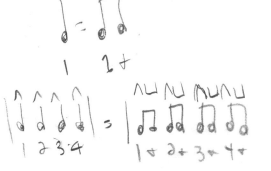

You already know this one. Again, when you do it, play the quarter notes as down-strokes and the groups of eighth notes as down-ups.

John Hardy

One of the great outlaw ballads that has found its way into bluegrass is frequently played as an instrumental. Look for the repeating phrases, which will make the tune easier to learn. Once you have it down, try increasing your speed just a bit, always making sure you keep it smooth.

Possible difficulties

Now that you know a few tunes, and are beginning to feel at home with the mandolin, take a little time to see whether you have any problems that need attention. The difficulties listed below are probably the most common:

Jerky, uneven sound. This can result from failing to keep a steady rhythm going with the foot, from gripping the pick too tightly or from moving the right hand too forcefully or too far. (It's sometimes hard to be completely objective about your smoothness—ask a friend to tell you if your playing sounds even.)

If you still experience problems, recheck your fingering. Following the rules on which finger to use for which fret (page 11) makes for the most efficient movement from one note to the next. If different fingers are used it can interrupt the flow of your playing.

The other major factor affecting smoothness is pick direction. Make sure you aren't playing certain notes as downstrokes when they should be upstrokes, or vice versa.

Tone poor and/or excessive pick noise. Gripping the pick too tightly or failing to keep it parallel with the strings can be responsible. Playing too close to the bridge will also produce this effect.

Arm or hand tired or cramped. Concentrating hard on something new can cause all sorts of muscles to tense up. Again, don't grip the pick too tightly, and don't use more force than necessary to press the strings against the fingerboard. In addition, check to be sure you are holding the strings down with the very tips of your fingers.

Shake out your right hand, letting it flop around from the wrist. Play a few down-up strokes on an open string while keeping hand and arm muscles as relaxed as possible. Then play one of the easier tunes and check yourself from time to time and see whether you are still really relaxed.

Picking double strings

The mandolin is by no means limited to single string melodies like the tunes you have learned so far. It is also well suited to playing a melody on one string and, simultaneously, a harmony part on another string. (Usually the harmony part is played on the next higher string above the melody.)

The downstroke

Try playing the first two strings (the 2nd and 1st strings) open as a single downstroke. Both pairs of each string should vibrate equally. Make sure that your attack is sharp enough so that all strings sound as one. Don't let the 1st string be heard a fraction of a second after the 2nd string. Repeat the downstroke until it sounds smooth and clean. Then try it on the middle two strings (3rd and 2nd strings) and finally on the lowest two (4th and 3rd).

The down-up stroke

In playing the down-up stroke on double strings, the main objective is to get the up-stroke to sound identical to the downstroke which precedes it. Both proper pick angle (as discussed in the later section on the *right hand*) and holding the pick loosely are extremely important.

Play the first two strings (2nd string and 1st string) together with a series of slow, smooth down-up strokes. Don't let the 1st string be heard louder than the 2nd string on the upstroke. Make sure that both 2nd and 1st strings sound simultaneously, whether on the down or upstroke. As you gain control, try playing a little faster, always retaining your smoothness. Now, try the same thing on the other pairs of adjacent strings.

The slide, the tremolo, and hammering-on

Both the slide and the tremolo can be done on double strings by applying the double string technique described above to the points covered in the earlier sections on these items. Hammering-on is generally done on just one string, but a double string effect is achieved when two strings are picked and one of the two is hammered.

Boil Em Cabbage Down, Part I

(Melody on the high strings)

This is a standard mountain fiddle tune that works well on the mandolin. It can be played on double strings throughout, as in the following version:

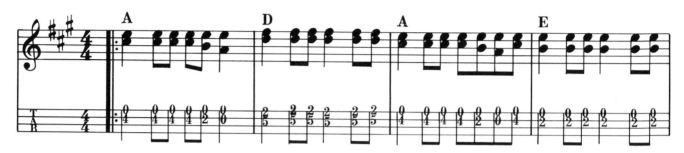

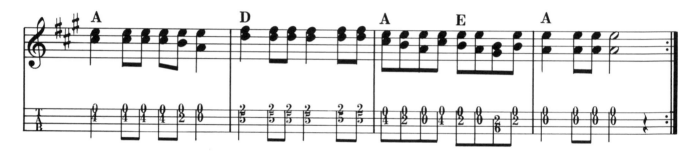

Notice that measures 1 and 2 are identical to measures 5 and 6. Measure 3 is similar to measures 1 and 5, only more complex.

Be sure to get measure 7 well under control. The last two notes are played with the first finger at the 2nd string, 2nd fret and the third finger at the 3rd string, 6th fret. If this is a hard stretch to make, practice it separately a few times. Playing this measure apart from the rest of the tune will also help.

Boil Em Cabbage Down, Part II A

(Melody on the low strings)

This will give you additional practice making the stretch between the 2nd and 6th frets. In measures 2 and 6, play the 4th string, 7th fret with the *third* finger and the 3rd string, 4th fret with the *first* finger. Use the normal fingering everywhere else.

Measure 8 consists of both 4th and 3rd strings noted at the 2nd fret. These may be noted in any of three ways:

a. One fingertip covering both strings. If your fingertips are large and your strings are fairly close together, you may be able to put your finger between the 4th and 3rd strings, noting in the usual manner, and hold them both down.

b. Two fingers. You may use the first and second fingers, one on each string.

c. Barre. You may press the last joint of the first finger flat against the fingerboard, holding both strings down.

a   b   c

As in Part I, measures 1 and 2 are the same as measures 5 and 6, and measure 3 is also
the same as measure 1.

Boil Em Cabbage Down, Part II B

(Rhythmic variation)

Instead of just repeating Part IIA a second time, let's try a variation on the rhythm.
Part IIB is identical to IIA except for the following two measures:

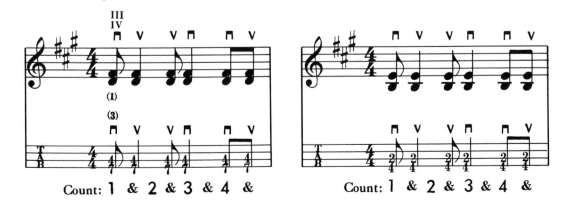

Count: 1 & 2 & 3 & 4 &   Count: 1 & 2 & 3 & 4 &

As the pick direction symbols indicate, these phrases are exceptions to the rule that quarter notes are played as downstrokes.

Here's why. When you play a measure of eight eighth notes, your pick direction is:

	down	up	down	up	down	up	down	up
Count:	1	&	2	&	3	&	4	&

In the measures shown above for Part IIB we have just removed the eighth notes from two of the beats, as follows:

	down	up	down	up	down	up	down	up
Count:	1	&	2	&	3	&	4	&

Pick direction remains the same as it would have been had all the eighth notes been used, and the rhythm of your right hand continues smoothly.

After you can do the measures shown above, try putting them into the tune, as given below. As always, *be sure to keep the count even.*

Now that you have the individual parts of *Boil Em Cabbage Down,* play the entire tune through. Part I is played twice (as indicated by the repeat sign); Part IIA, once; and Part IIB once.

You can go through this sequence as many times as you like. Square dance fiddlers think nothing of playing a tune for 15 or 20 minutes, though you may feel two or three times through is sufficient.

Using chords

Basic major chord positions. The mandolin is nearly always played in combination with at least one other instrument, normally a guitar. In a bluegrass band there is also likely to be a banjo, fiddle and bass, and perhaps a dobro as well. When the mandolin is not playing the lead part (as in the tunes we've covered thus far) it must accompany vocals or other lead instruments. Chording is the simplest and most common way of playing accompaniment.

The most important chord to master is the G chord shown below:

(The numbers in the diagram show which fingers to use.)

You may find using the fourth finger to hold down the 7th fret of the 4th string is rather awkward at first. With time, however, your fingers will gain in flexibility, and it will come to feel natural.

Once you can make the G chord, the C chord will present no great problem. It can be played in either of the two ways shown below:

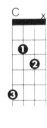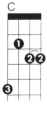

("X" indicates a string not played.)

The version on the right is the more complete of the two, as only three strings are played in the other variation. The size of your fingers and the distance between strings on your mandolin will determine whether you can hold both 1st and 2nd strings at the 3rd fret with the tip of your second finger. (Trying to flatten out the finger for this purpose is normally not effective.)

If you use the three string version of C, try deadening the 1st string with the second finger which is noting the 2nd string at the 3rd fret. Rock your finger back against the 1st string just enough so that when struck with the pick, the string produces a dull thud instead of a note. (The reason for doing this will be apparent later.)

When you practice a chord, first play each individual string, one at a time. If one string sounds dead or buzzes, stop and find out why. The most likely possibilities are:

1. Your finger is not close enough to the fret
2. Your finger is on top of the fret
3. The string needs to be held tighter
4. Another finger is inadvertently touching the string and deadening it.

Once the individual chords sound well by themselves, practice changing from one chord to another, still playing each one a string at a time to make sure all the notes are clear. When you shift from G to C, lift your fourth finger off the 4th string, then move your other three fingers as a unit. Each finger ends up noting the next lower string at the same fret it held down in the G chord. In changing from C back to G, the process is just reversed.

Two other important chords, A and D are shown below:

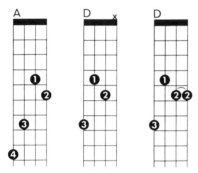

Notice that they are identical to G and C respectively, except that they are played two frets higher. After you feel comfortable with these chords, try the following changes:

1. A to D to A
2. G to D to G
3. D to G to A to D

Playing chords as accompaniment. Make a G chord. Play the 4th string as a downstroke with your pick. Now brush sharply across all four strings so they sound as though all are being struck simultaneously.

The rhythm is like this:

Count:	1	&	2	&	3	&	4	&
	4th string		brush		4th string		brush	

Written out, this would be:

Count: 1 & 2 & 3 & 4 &

Each stroke falls on the count of "1", "2", "3", or "4". Nothing is played on the "&" 's.

Now, instead of letting the chord ring after you play the brush stroke, try cutting the sound off abruptly to produce a staccato sound. To do this, relax the fingers of your left hand just enough to deaden the strings a split second after you complete the brush stroke. The result will be the "oom-*cha,* oom-*cha*" offbeat rhythm frequently heard on bluegrass recordings.

(When playing with another instrument some players omit hitting the 4th string on beats 1 and 3 leaving only the brush strokes on beats 2 and 4.)

Additional major chords. Any major chord can be played by moving the G and C formations you have already learned to the proper fret. Other frequently used chords are given below:

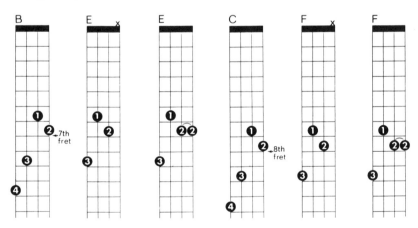

You can now play accompaniment for the tunes we have covered so far. Try them, one at a time, following the chord symbols given over the tablature line, and playing two repetitions of the 4th string-brush sequence per measure. When you try them, be sure, as always, that you choose a speed sufficiently slow so that the rhythm is even and without interruption at the hard spots—that is, where the chord changes occur.

Four fiddle tunes

Fiddle tunes have always been an important component of country and bluegrass music. Since a fiddle is tuned to the same notes as a mandolin, most fiddle pieces are readily adaptable to the mandolin.

The following tunes are among the best-known mountain hoedowns. Though they have long been used for square dancing, bluegrass musicians often pace them a good bit faster than dance tempo

Old Joe Clark

The fingers of your left hand keep pretty busy in this tune; you will soon feel comfortable with it if you learn it as a series of phrases, several of which recur two or three times.

In the tenth measure you will slide your third finger to the 7th fret of the 2nd string, playing that string and also the first string open. Since the 2nd string, 7th fret, produces the same note as the 1st string open, it may seem odd to play both notes together. However, as a little experimentation will show you, their combined sound is considerably stronger and more satisfying at this point in the song than either string played by itself would be.

In playing these notes, though, and in playing double strings elsewhere in tunes which are played mostly on single strings, be careful not to overplay. Two strings produce twice as much sound as one, and if you bear down hard on them, the following passage on single strings may sound weak by comparison.

The ending is a different matter. You normally want the last notes of an up-tempo tune to be as strong or stronger than what has preceded them. You can thus play a bit harder on the last two notes of the ending for a strong finale.

Soldier's Joy

The tricky part in this one is the rhythm in measures two, four and six. In each case the rhythm is the same as in measures two, four and six of *Boil Em Cabbage Down,* Part IIB. In *Soldier's Joy,* however, you are also changing from one note to another in the course of the phrase. Be careful to keep the correct pick direction as well as to play the rhythm properly:

Count: 1 & 2 & 3 & 4 &

When you have the above measure down, try the full tune:

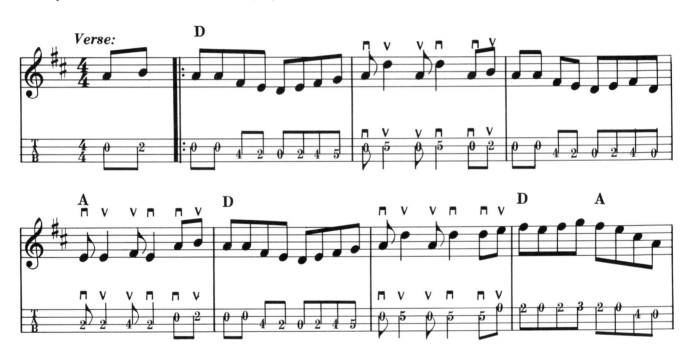

Cripple Creek

Your hand is moved up the neck at the start of this one. In the first measure your second finger will be noting the 1st string, 5th fret; your first finger will note the 2nd string, 4th fret.

In the second measure your hand shifts again so that your first finger plays the 2nd string, 5th fret, and your third finger hits the 2nd string, 9th fret. The open strings that follow give you plenty of time to shift back down to your normal hand position for the third measure.

Notice the repeating phrase in the third and fourth measures. It is an odd length—just 3/4 of a measure—and it's set off between dotted lines to point this out. Make sure you play straight through both repetitions without pausing.

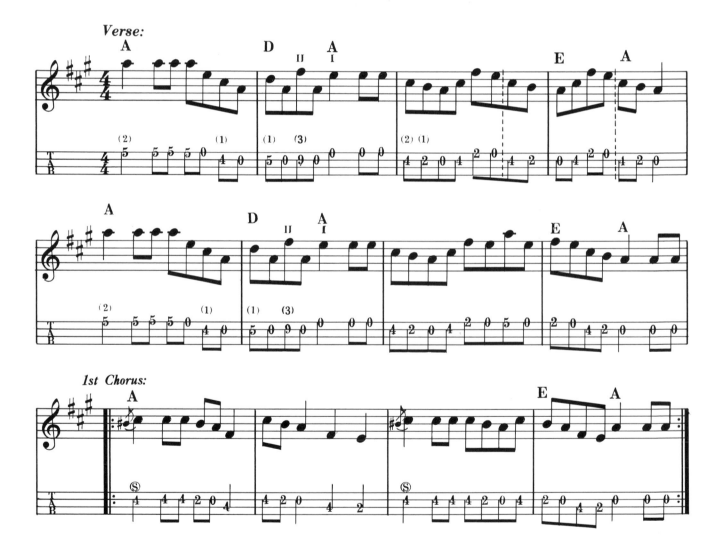

For variety, try an alternate way of playing the chorus, based on the repeating phrase mentioned above. The deceptive rhythm is a variation of a type of fiddle shuffle, and it is this rhythm rather than the melody which gives this section its impact. Since the phrases move in and out of the phase with the beat of the tune, be sure to keep your foot tapping and your down-up strokes controlled and even.

As in the verse of *Cripple Creek* the dotted lines in the music are just to show you how the phrases are made up; don't let them affect the timing of your down-up strokes through the unbroken series of eighth notes.

When you can play the various parts of the tune individually, put them together as follows:

1. Verse
2. First chorus
3. Verse (same as first time)
4. Second chorus
5. Ending

Arkansas Traveller

This tune requires still more shifting up the neck and back down again. When shifting, be particularly careful to use the correct fingers as indicated in parentheses above the tablature line. Also, be sure to play the tune slowly enough so that you don't have to pause while doing the shifts.

Instrumental breaks

A variety of approaches in various keys.

In bluegrass, as in many other musical styles, songs are not just for singers. Singing is, of course, an extremely important part of any song. But in bluegrass a great emphasis has come to be placed on the instrumental sections in vocal numbers. (In rock or jazz these are referred to as *solos* when they feature a single instrument; bluegrass musicians call them *breaks*.) A bluegrass audience rarely interrupts a song by clapping for a vocal section, but a hot instrumental break in the proper context will often provoke enthusiastic cheers and applause.

Vocals and instrumental breaks are generally integrated into a song according to some variation on the following pattern:

a. Kickoff   *Instrumental introduction*
b. 1st verse   *Vocal*
c. Chorus   *Vocal*
d. Break   *Instrumental*
e. 2nd verse   *Vocal*
f. Chorus   *Vocal*
g. Break   *Instrumental*
h. 3rd verse   *Vocal*
i. Chorus   *Vocal*

Numerous versions of this idea exist, depending on the number of verses, the tempo of the song, etc., but the pattern of vocal sections alternating in some manner with instrumental ones is followed in the vast majority of bluegrass songs. The kickoff may be equivalent to a full verse of the song, or it may be just a few measures of music. The same instrument may play all the breaks, or each break may feature a different instrument. Sometimes two instruments will each take half of a given break. Occasionally they may split it up into still smaller segments.

One of the exciting aspects of bluegrass is the great diversity of ways in which the break for any given song may be played. The break may consist of nearly the same notes as those sung by the vocalist. Or, it may take the basic vocal melody, and add embellishments or ornaments here and there. Sometimes the basic melody may be modified to the point where it sounds like a different, though related, tune. And it is even possible to play a totally unrelated alternate melody whose only kinship with the vocal is that is still works with the chord pattern of the song.

How straight or how far out a break is played depends on the individual musician, his ability and his taste. The best breaks, however, are not necessarily the fanciest. Whether simple or complex, they are the ones which best complement the song and the arrangement within which they are played.

This chapter contains a number of widely played bluegrass songs in different keys and a variety of breaks for them. Notice that the chord pattern for the break is always the same as the chord pattern of the song. (However, certain breaks may have an extra measure on the beginning for a short introductory phrase.)

As you go through each break, whether simple or complex, think of the song while you play. Once you know where the notes of the break fall, listen to how they relate to the corresponding vocal phrases.

(You will find that some of the accompanying chords are new to you. A glance at Appendix VII will show how to play them using the G and C formations you already know.)

To start, let's try a tune that can be done either in slow or at medium tempo.

Banks of the Ohio

Verses:
I held a knife against her breast
As into my arms she pressed
Cried "Oh Willie don't murder me
For I am unprepared to die."

Going home at half past one
Crying, "God, what have I done
Killed the only one I love
Because she would not marry me."

Chorus:
And only say that you'll be mine
In our home we'll happy be
Out beside where the waters flow
Down by the banks of the Ohio.

Here is a straightforward break on single strings which follows the melody quite closely throughout. When you hammer-on, be sure the note comes out sharp and clear. (If you wish, you can learn the break without hammering-on and add it later.)

45

Nearly the same melody can be readily played on double strings, though it means playing up the neck in some places to get the appropriate harmony notes.

Pretty Polly

Pretty Polly is quite a powerful mountain ballad. Certain notes in the melody generate an exciting tension when heard against the major chord accompaniment. (The notes for the vocal line and for the breaks are the same ones heard often in rock music and referred to as falling within a "blues scale".)

Vocal:

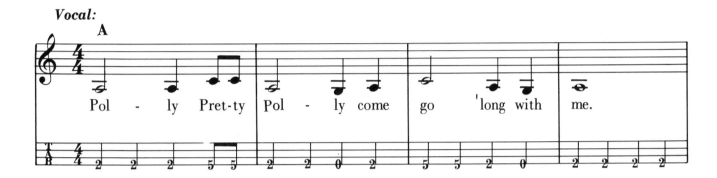

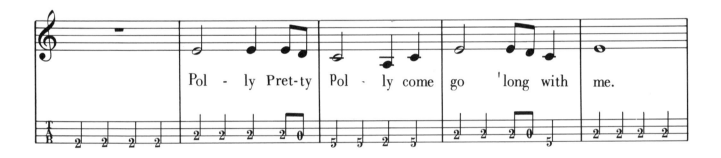

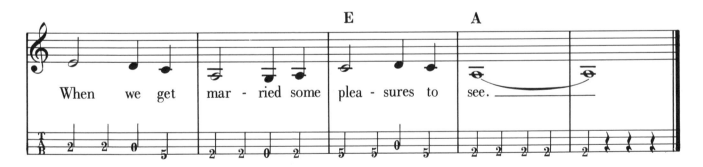

Verses:
Willie, oh Willie I'm afraid of your ways
Willie, oh Willie I'm afraid of your ways
The way that you ramble you'll lead me astray.

He led her over mountains and valleys so deep
He led her over mountains and valleys so deep
Polly mistrusted and began for to weep.

He opened her bosom as white as the snow
He opened her bosom as white as the snow
He stabbed her to the heart and her heart's blood did flow.

Gentlemen and ladies I bid you farewell
Gentlemen and ladies I bid you farewell
Killing Pretty Polly will send my soul to hell.

The first break, which is played entirely on the two lowest strings, stays close to the melody.

In measure 12, you will play an open third string, followed by the 4th string, 5th fret. If the 3rd string continues to ring even after you hit the following note, the two notes will clash somewhat. Should this occur, you can deaden the string by touching it with your first finger at the same time you note the fourth string with your third finger.

Low Strings:

The next break for *Pretty Polly* is a bit more brilliant as it is played chiefly on the two highest strings. The latter part of the melody is heavily ornamented.

At the beginning of measure 2, notice that you play a downstroke on the 2nd string followed by an upstroke on the 3rd, which may feel a little awkward. Make sure the second note of the measure sounds just as strong as the first.

When you come to measure 10, accent the last note of the measure slightly. Also be sure you give the quarter rest in measure 11 its correct value. Done properly the effect is that of an ear-catching syncopation.

Careless Love

This song is typical in its chord progression of the way a great many bluegrass songs are put together.

Guitar: Capo at 3rd Fret

Verses:
Love my Mom and Daddy too
Love my Mom and Daddy too
Love my Mom and my Daddy too
I'll leave them both to be with you.

On this lonesome rail I stand
On this lonesome rail I stand
On this lonesome rail I stand
Thinking about my railroad man.

The first break consists of an ornamented version of the melody.

In measure 11 the first finger of the left hand notes the 1st string, 1st fret and then moves to the 2nd fret.

*The chords in parentheses are to be played by the guitar when the capo is used as indicated.

The next break is played up the neck, although the melody is modified to move from a high range to a medium one, and then back to the high one.

Playing measure 10 and continuing into measure 11 may be easier if you notice that you are moving up the neck on two strings chromatically, that is, one fret at a time. On the 1st and 2nd strings you start at the 4th and 8th frets respectively. You then move to the 5th and 9th frets and finally end up at the 6th and 10th frets.

Guitar: Capo at 3rd Fret.

Modified Melody:

Nine Pound Hammer

This tune is sometimes done fast, but more often at a medium speed with a good deal of push.

Guitar: Capo at 4th Fret.

Verses:

There ain't no hammer on this mountain
Rings like mine, that rings like mine.

Rings like silver, and shines like gold
Rings like silver, and it shines like gold.

Somebody stole my nine pound hammer
And they took it and gone, Lord they took it and
  gone.

Well, I'm going on the mountain to see my baby
And I ain't coming back, Lord I ain't coming back.

The first break is fairly straight. Be sure to keep the standard down-up pattern through-out, especially in measure 5. (When you have a downstroke on the 2nd string followed by an upstroke on the first string, there may sometimes be a tendency to play both as downstrokes. Don't let this happen, as it will throw off your timing until you return to the correct picking pattern.)

The last note of measure 9 is another example of a string which should not be allowed to ring once the following note is played. As in the first *Pretty Polly* break, deaden it with your first finger, if necessary, as you play the next note.

The second break gets pretty far out. It consists of an alternate melody that does not at all resemble the tune, yet, in some way retains an identification with the song.

Notice the x's in measures 10 and 11. These indicate that you still hit the strings with the pick, but that you deaden them so that in place of a note, only a percussive *click* is heard. The deadening is accomplished the same way you damp a chord: relax your finger on the string slightly so that you are no longer holding it tight against the fret.

The normal down-up pick sequence is preserved throughout these two measures, and the notes which are played in the usual manner jump out at unexpected times from among the deadened notes. Be sure that the fourth note in measure 10 and the second note in measure 11 are each played, as shown, on the upstroke.

In measure 12 the usual down-up pattern *is* altered, so be sure you keep the timing steady. Each slide from the 5th to the 6th fret takes the same time as if you picked both notes. Instead you are picking the note at the 5th fret and moving your finger up one more fret to produce the higher note. The count is as follows:

Jack Tottle.

Now try the break:

Guitar; Capo at 4th Fret.
Alternate Melody:

Jesse James

Jesse James must be the most widely sung of the old outlaw ballads. It's another song that can be done either as a vocal or as an instrumental.

Verses:

They say his brother Frank had robbed the Gallatin bank
And taken the money from the town
It was at that very place they had a little race
Where they shot Captain Sheets to the ground.

It was Robert Ford, that lone little coward
I wonder what he does feel
Though he'd eat of Jesse's bread and he'd sleep in Jesse's bed
Still he laid poor Jesse in his grave.

It was on a summer's night when Jesse stayed at home
With his loving wife so brave
Robert Ford came in like a thief from the night
And laid poor Jesse in his grave.

Four different breaks for *Jesse James* are given to illustrate how various approaches we've examined can apply to a given song. They'll be an asset to your repertoire as well; how often do we hear, even on record, a mandolin player take four distinctively different breaks in the same song?

The straight break on single strings should present no difficulty:

Single Strings:

Repeat the 2nd and 3rd lines above, then continue:

The straight melody using double strings requires special attention only at a couple of transitions from up the neck back down to your basic first position.

In measure number 16, as you note the 5th and 7th frets with your 2nd and 3rd fingers respectively, also place your first finger on the 2nd string, 4th fret. In that way you don't need to find your place when you remove your 2nd and 3rd fingers.

Repeat the 2nd and 3rd lines above, then continue:

This next break is an ornamented version of the melody. The open 4th string in measure 20 may sound unusual when you play it slowly. When you play it up to speed, it will sound perfectly normal.

Repeat the 2nd and 3rd lines above, then continue:

The alternate melody below has a good deal of picking well up the neck. Learn it slowly and carefully with, as always, attention to pick direction and you'll sound very impressive playing it.

Alternate Melody

Repeat the 2nd and 3rd lines above, then continue:

The fourth finger

So far we've used the fourth finger only in chords. Now it's time to look at using it to play melodies.

With your hand in basic first position, note the 1st string, 2nd fret using your first finger. Without moving your first finger, note the 1st string, 7th fret using your fourth finger.

Whether or not this is a difficult stretch depends on the size and flexibility of your hand, and the strength of your fingers. While hand size is pretty much predetermined for you, the more you use your fourth finger, the greater its strength and flexibility will become.

With your hand in the position described above, look at your fourth finger. Are all the joints bent convex as mentioned in the earlier section on the left hand? Or has one of the joints locked or straightened out?

right   wrong

While a certain amount of use can be gotten from the fourth finger even if it does straighten out, you can use it much more quickly and accurately by learning to keep it bent.

Hand position can have alot to do with this. Often moving the hand until it is just a little more nearly parallel with the neck will help. As the part of the left hand where the fourth finger joins it approaches the neck of the mandolin more closely, the fourth finger, when placed on a string, is forced to bend outward instead of straightening out.

Experiment until you find a position that works, but be sure not to cramp or twist your hand radically in the process. Don't be impatient; over a period of time control of your fourth finger will improve in proportion to the amount you use it.

Exercises

Before using the fourth finger in a tune, try the first exercise given below. It simply takes you up through a series of notes known as a scale, and brings you back down without the use of open strings.

Play it first slowly and evenly, as written, using all downstrokes:

The G Scale

Now, another exercise with slightly different intervals:

The A Scale

Warming up with these at an easy, comfortable pace each time you play will be good practice for your fourth finger. When you start feeling at home with them, try playing them with down-up strokes, as if they were written using eighth notes.

Red-Haired Boy

Red-haired Boy is a good tune for putting your fourth finger to work.

The rhythm in the first measure (and in measures 5 and 14 which are identical to it) is the same found in *Boil Em Cabbage Down,* Part IIB (measures 2, 4 and 6) and in *Soldier's Joy* (measures 2, 4, and 6) so be sure your pick direction and timing are the same as in those tunes.

Practice measures 1 and 2 together until the shift up the neck and the use of the fourth finger come easily. Then try the tune.

To add further interest, let's try varying certain phrases, while preserving the rest of the melody intact. The two measures given below can be substituted in place of measures 3 and 4 or of measures 12 and 13:

Variation 1:

So can the following two measures:

Variation 2:

And also these two:

Variation 3:

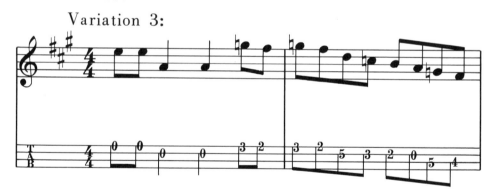

The above phrases can be integrated into the tune in any of several ways. Try the tune with variations as outlined below. Then, if you like, rearrange the order according to your own choice.

a.	Verse	*Straight*
b.	Verse	*Straight*
c.	Chorus	*Straight*
d.	Chorus	*Straight*
e.	Verse	*Using variation 1*
f.	Verse	*Using variation 2*
g.	Chorus	*Using variation 3*
h.	Chorus	*Using variation 3*
i.	Ending	

Fisher's Hornpipe

Part I is the melody. Check out the fingering in measures 2-3 and 13-14 and be sure you can play them readily before you start the tune. The chords change twice per measure throughout much of the tune which means playing just one repetition of the 4th string/brush stroke accompaniment before moving on to the next chord.

In *Red-Haired Boy* the variations were devised to preserve the original melody while altering certain phrases. Part II of *Fisher's Hornpipe* does just the opposite. A minor melody with a very different feel is superimposed against the tune's rapid major chord changes. The points in common with the original will probably not be apparent until you get used to the new sound.

Minor Variation

* Slide is from 5th fret.

Sailor's Hornpipe

Some of us first heard this tune as background for Popeye cartoon movies, but it makes a great bluegrass piece. It also provides a real workout for your fourth finger. Practice measures 6 and 7 separately before you try the full tune.

Pick direction is the usual down-up through-out. Pay particular attention to keep this when you get to measures 8, 11 and 13 as well as to the ending.

70

Consolidating your progress

By now you have learned a sizeable number of tunes. You are pretty much at home in the basic first position and you can play up the neck as well. You have played melodies on single strings and on double strings, simple melodies and complex ones. You know how to use chords, and your fourth finger is starting to become a part of your melody work.

How do you sound? As noted earlier, objectivity about your own playing is a tough proposition. The idea is to recognize the areas in which a little extra thought can help bring out into the open the knowledge and skills you have already gained.

Solid timing is still the most fundamental point; listen hard for it. Can you tap your foot in a rock steady rhythm while you play even the very most demanding passages you know?

At this stage, maybe not. But once you have these passages down really cold, they won't seem exceptionally difficult and you will want to be able to tap through them. (This is the key to solid control over tunes with tricky timing, such as the second break to *Nine Pound Hammer.*) On any tune which you consider you have fully mastered, be sure you can keep the rhythm in this way, with no speeding up or slowing down.

How is your pick? Does it tend to catch in the strings at times? Do your notes played on the upstroke come out with equal crispness and clarity to your downstrokes, especially on double strings? Do you sometimes feel a sense of fighting your way across the strings when you pick them?

If your playing is not completely smooth yet, you are probably still gripping the pick too tightly. Reread the previous sections on the right hand and on relaxing it. It's very easy to start out a song quite relaxed and to unconsciously tighten up little by little as you go along until by the end, you have the pick in a death lock. Check for this as often as necessary, and make it a regular part of your playing until you are sure your picking is completely fluid, even and smooth.

Though the emphasis thus far has been on slow steady playing, you have doubtless noticed that much of bluegrass music is played fairly fast. Once you are confident that you have achieved good timing and smoothness you can begin working on your speed. When you feel you're ready, pick one of the easiest tunes you know and try it slightly faster than usual. Lighten your touch a bit, but don't let any sloppiness creep into the tune. If it works at this speed, try another little increase in tempo the next time around. (Don't, however, speed up part way through.)
Take care that in your eagerness to keep up with your favorite bluegrass record, you don't overreach yourself. Stay with the easier tunes as you gradually build up speed, and keep them clean as a whistle.

Playing with other people

Bluegrass as a group effort.

Bluegrass is, by definition, a music played by two or more people. Playing along with the instruction record is good practice for getting the feel of playing with other instruments. If you have a tape recorder or cassette, you can record yourself playing the melody to a tune and then play the accompanying chords as you listen to the playback. (This can be of considerable help in checking how evenly and smoothly you are playing.)

Nevertheless, you will want at some point to start looking for like-minded individuals to play with. If none of your friends are into music, notes on the bulletin boards at your local record store, music store, high school, or college student union are likely to bring results. You could also contact a couple of guitar or banjo teachers to find out if any of their bluegrass students would like to jam with you.

Playing with other people can be wonderfully stimulating and exciting, but it does require some thought. Bluegrass is played most successfully in small groups of around three to six people. When you are starting out, the smaller the group size, the more manageable it will be. A guitar is essential. Banjo, fiddle and/or dobro will work in any combination. A bass will add greatly to the solidity of whatever sized group you have.

Get in tune carefully at the beginning. Playing when someone is out of tune is like trying to swim up Niagara Falls—no matter how much effort you put out, the results are highly disappointing.

The overriding rule in playing with others is miraculously simple: *Listen.* While you will naturally have to focus much of your attention on making sure you are playing the right chords, notes, etc., work simultaneously at hearing what is going on around you.

When you play a break, listen to the rhythm set up by the other instruments, especially the guitar and (if there is one) the bass. They are responsible for setting you up with a strong solid beat. You, in turn, must merge with it, neither pulling ahead nor dragging behind.

When you are backing up a vocalist or another instrument, you can devote still more of your attention to listening, and you'll need to. You are now responsible for playing solidly with the guitar, bass and other instruments to make whoever is out front sound good.

While you are playing accompaniment can you hear clearly what the lead vocalist or instrumentalist is doing? If not, either you or someone else is playing too loud. (There is nothing less conducive to enjoyment or to good music than devoting your full energies to being heard above the din created by your fellow musicians. "Do unto others . . .")

Backing a vocalist

1. With chords. The accompaniment with chords you have learned works equally well behind vocals as it does backing up instrumental breaks. It is the most usual type of accompaniment, and will not clash with the vocal as long as it is played at the correct volume. (Normally you will chord a bit more quietly behind vocals than instrumentals, but the offbeat chop should always be solid and clean.)

2. With chords plus fill-in phrases. On slow or medium-paced songs it is possible to vary the straight chording by inserting short phrases in between vocal lines. The phrases given below will work in the vocal version of *Pretty Polly*.

Fill-in # 1:

Fill-in # 2:

Try singing (or humming) the first verse of *Pretty Polly* and inserting Fill-in 1 after the first vocal line, and Fill-in 2 at the end of the last line.

Compare your version with the following one. This one also includes the second verse, with a couple of additional fill-ins.

Pretty Polly

Accompaniment with Fill-ins:

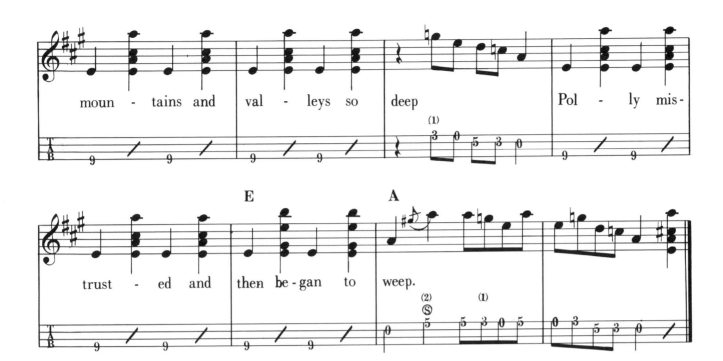

moun - tains and val - leys so deep Pol - ly mis-

E   A

trust - ed and then be - gan to weep.

When you do the entire song try playing a couple of verses with fill-ins, then a couple with straight chords only, then another two with fill-ins, etc. This keeps the song from getting too predictable, and also gives the opportunity for another instrument to fill in when you don't.

3. Melodically. It is possible to play melody notes throughout a vocal section under certain circumstances, but unless a player is highly skilled this is likely to detract from, rather than support, the singer. There is already an overabundance of bluegrass aficionados who massage their egos by playing endless melodic passages through each verse and chorus of any song, with no concern for the overall sound. One such superstar in a group is torture. Two or more create utter chaos.

One way to play melodically behind a singer in a supportive role is to play in harmony to his or her voice. This can be the same part that a second voice would sing if the song were a duet. The following example shows how this would work for *Banks of the Ohio.*

The Lilly Brothers, Everett and Bea.

Banks of the Ohio

Notice that the fill-in at the next to last measure comes directly from the version of *Wildwood Flower* found earlier in the book. There are, of course, plenty of different ways to construct this kind of fill-in. A couple of other ways to play the last two measures are shown below.

When you play the song, you can provide additional interest by varying the fill-ins from verse to verse. If you can come up with additional fill-ins on your own, so much the better.

Backing other lead instruments

When another lead instrument is playing a break, you will normally play straight chords. Inserting fill-ins is likely to work only if the lead instrument pauses (or, in the case of the fiddle, holds a long note) specifically to let another instrument add something.

Let the volume of the lead instrument determine how loud you play. A banjo is normally the loudest lead instrument; the fiddle is usually of medium volume. Be careful backing the dobro, and most especially the guitar since these are the two quietest instruments. You may find that for the guitar leads to be heard you are only able to lightly brush across the strings when you chop chords behind it.

As with accompanying vocals, however, two instruments can play a break together, provided both musicians know what they are doing. Just playing a mandolin break while the banjo is taking its break sounds even worse than playing heedlessly through a vocal section. But two instruments playing in harmony can be extremely powerful musically and are fun for the musicians.

The piece below is the harmony part for the version of *Red-haired Boy* you have already learned. The harmony version sounds a bit strange when heard by itself, and it is not designed to be used except with another instrument playing the melody part.
The melody you know can be played exactly as it is on another mandolin or on the fiddle. A guitar or banjo can also play the same melody, though the fingering will be totally different.

If you have access to a tape recorder you can play the tune as a duet with yourself. Record yourself playing the melody version. Then, as you listen to the playback, do the harmony version along with it. The effect will startle you.

Red-Haired Boy

Lead mandolin playing

1. Breaks. When you play a break, or, for that matter, an instrumental piece, bear in mind that the most noticeable things you do will be the first and last phrases you play. Come into your break confidently, and finish it cleanly. (There are few things as anti-climactic as a strong instrumental which concludes by fluffing the last couple of notes.)

During your break, think of playing with feeling. Be conscious of the lyrics to the song. The mood the singer uses them to create should determine whether your break is played sweetly or aggressively, loud or soft. Playing part of a break softly and building to a pushy and strong finish can sometimes be very striking. There are numerous instances where a simple and mellow break can make a song successful where a fancy break would destroy it.

2. Kickoffs. The instrumental introduction to a song may be a full length break, but it doesn't always have to be. On exceptionally long songs in particular, it is often desirable to introduce the tune with something shorter.

In *Banks of the Ohio* (from either page 45 or 46) for example, you could readily open with the equivalent of half a verse. You would start with measure 9 (omitting the first note of the measure) and play through to the end of the break

Or, you could shorten it still further to just one quarter of the verse. To do this, you would begin instead with measure 13 (again omitting the first note). An introduction shorter than half a verse is called a *turnaround*.

Turnarounds are also used in place of instrumental breaks within songs, most often in slow ones. Many bluegrass gospel recordings, especially the older ones, use turnarounds almost exclusively.

3. Endings. Songs can be wrapped up with tag endings of the type we have done on the various fiddle tunes. Most often, however, the mandolin joins the other instruments in a simple rhythmic riff on the final chord. A couple of the most common ones are shown below. (These are written in A, but they work the same way in any chord. The chords in the tablature line are spelled out by string and fret instead of with the slash mark to show better how the down and upstrokes fall.)

Ending #1:

Ending #2:

The ending normally begins on the last vocal note. Thus, in *Banks of the Ohio,* we would play:

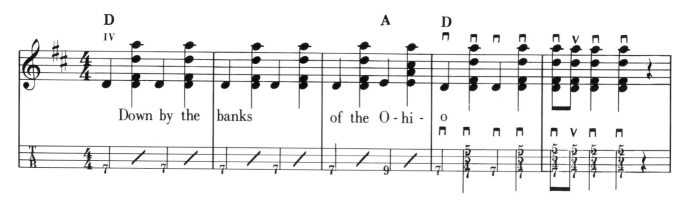

The final chord can be clipped off by damping it or it can be allowed to ring, according to your preference for any given song. It will be most effective if everyone in the group treats it the same, whether damping it or letting it fade out by itself.

Some songs lend themselves to a slowdown in tempo right at the end, usually around a measure or two before the last vocal note.

Try the ending for *Pretty Polly* as written below. As you sing the word *send* the tempo slows abruptly. The time elapsed between each beat and the next then becomes progressively longer until the last note is sung. The final fill-in phrase on the mandolin flows out of the last vocal note and then dies away.

Playing with others you are bound to hear new musical ideas, and, in the process, gain new insights into the potential of your own instrument. In the absence of orchestrated scores detailing exactly how each instrument should play throughout a given tune (which would take a good bit of joy out of playing anyhow) you are forced into a certain amount of experimentation. This chapter has covered some of the options open to you, but there is no way it could deal with even a fraction of the total number of possibilities.

Having gone through the preceding examples, try not to be limited by them. If you can hum a little fill-in phrase, a turnaround or an ending, you can, with some diligent searching, find the right notes on your mandolin. It doesn't matter whether you (or anyone else) think your first efforts sound simple or clumsy. If you have to try ten different note combinations before you come up with a simple musical phrase that sounds acceptable, you're doing just fine. Keep it up and your average will get better and better.

The tremolo

As mentioned earlier, the tremolo is simply a rapid succession of down-up strokes. It can be done at any of several different speeds, but full control over the pick at the speed used is very important.

First, tap your foot at a moderate tempo and play a series of eighth notes on your open 2nd string:

Now, with your foot tapping *at exactly the same tempo,* double your number of pick strokes.

Tremolo # 1:

You now have 16 notes in the same space where you previously played eight.

Try slightly accenting the downstrokes which fall on the beats (number counts "1", "2", "3", and "4") to make sure your timing is even. You are thus accenting every fourth note you are picking, and the accented notes correspond to each downward tap of your foot. (The accenting is for practice purposes only. You won't normally want to do it when you play a break.)

Make sure you can do tremolo 1 well. Then, with your foot still tapping the same tempo used above, once again double your number of pick strokes:

Tremolo ♯ 2:

Count: 1   &   2   &   3   &   4   &

In the same time span that contained 16 notes when you played Tremolo 1, you now have 32 notes.

Accenting the downstroke on each beat—this time falling every eight notes, but still on each downward foot tap—will provide a check on your timing. When you can do this smoothly, you will have the basis of a good respectable tremolo.

Will the Circle Be Unbroken is a good tune on which to try out your tremolo.

Herchel Sizemore of Country Grass.

Sam Bush of the Newgrass Revival.

Will the Circle Be Unbroken

To start with, play the break given below ignoring the tremolo notation, that is, with the usual down-up strokes. Keep your first finger in place on the 3rd string, 5th fret, throughout except where you have to move it (for example to the 2nd string, 5th fret). Anchoring it in place while your other fingers play the 7th, 8th and 9th frets gives you a point of reference and eliminates unnecessary movement.

Will the Circle Be Unbroken

It would be possible to play the above break with an unbroken tremolo from start to finish. It adds variety, however, to intersperse tremolo passages with short phrases of quarter and eighth notes.

Try the slower of the two tremolos—Tremolo 1—first. You will thus be playing two notes (a down and upstroke) for each eighth note with a tremolo marking. Keep your foot tapping evenly, and be sure you are making the transition smoothly from tremolo to non-tremolo sections (that is, from measure 2 to 3; from the beginning of measure 5 to the end of that measure, etc.). Count out loud if you need to, but make sure these transitions are under control.

(By the way, slides work well with the tremolo, but hammering-on does not; just ignore the ⊕ symbols when playing tremoloed notes.)

After you have mastered the break with tremolo 1, double the speed of your tremolo, and try it with tremolo 2.

Again, be especially careful of the transitions out of the tremolo sections, and count aloud if you need to.

While most bluegrass can be written in 4/4 time (with four beats to the measure), there are a number of songs which have three beats to the measure. These are said to be in *3/4 time* or *waltz time.*

Accompaniment with chords is done by adding an extra downward brush stroke to the pattern you have used in 4/4 time. Try it with your D chord as shown below:

Songs in 3/4 time tend to be of slow or medium tempo, and the slower the song, the more likely a tremolo is to be used. *In the Pines* is a good example of a fairly slow tune in 3/4.

In the Pines

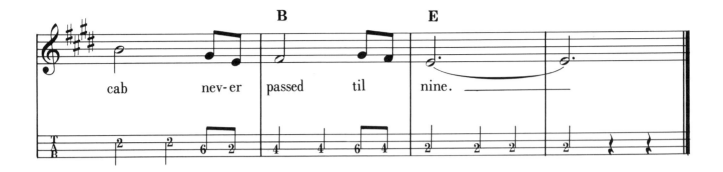

cab   nev-er   passed   til   nine. _____

As with the preceding song, try the break to *In the Pines* first without the tremolo, next with tremolo 1, and finally, once you understand the break fully, with tremolo 2.

Do this one slowly enough so that when you play the break without the tremolo you can use all downstrokes (despite the fact that most of it is written in eighth notes). When you add the tremolo, those phrases outside the tremolo sections will still be played with all downstrokes, enabling you to give each of these notes a firm emphasis.

One last item: tremolos 1 and 2 are not the only tremolos possible.
Depending on the tempo of a given song it may be possible to again double the
number of strokes in tremolo 2 resulting in 64 notes per 4/4 measure. This type
of tremolo, which we can call tremolo 3 is also often used in bluegrass, as it
approximates the sound of a single sustained note more closely than do the
slower tremolos.

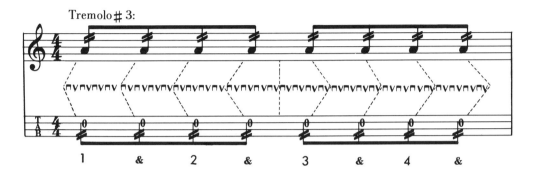

(Note: The measure above is spread out to facilitate showing how many
down-up strokes are used, but it should be thought of in the same tempo as the
earlier tremolo examples.)

Once you can play tremolos 1 and 2 well with the songs in this chapter, see
if you can phase tremolo 3 into your playing.

Marty Stuart and Kenny Ingraham. Marty began playing mandolin with Lester Flatt's Nashville Grass in his early teens.

Minors

Minor chords are relatively rare in traditional bluegrass. It may be this fact that makes them sound so dramatic when they are used.

Basic minor positions

Em and Am can be played as follows:

Notice that is both chords, the first finger flattens out to barre two strings simultaneously at the 2nd fret.

Moving these positions up the neck, as you have done with the major chords, you can form any minor chord.

When minor chords occur in bluegrass, it is usually within a tune in a major key—that is a tune that ends with a major chord.

Each key has one minor chord which is more closely associated with it than any other minor chord. This chord is called the *relative minor* of that key.

An expanded version of the *circle of fifths* shows the relative minor for each of the keys: (See Theory Lesson in appendix for description of circle of fifths)

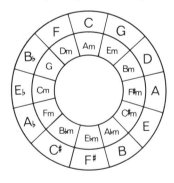

**Circle of Fifths
Showing Relative Minors**

The above diagram shows Am as the relative minor of C. This means that should a minor chord occur within a tune written in the key of C, that minor chord is most likely to be an A minor. Similarly, in the key of G, an E minor chord would be the minor most often used.

Joe Val with Dave Dillon of the New England Bluegrass Boys (top left), Frank Greathouse of the New Deal String Band (top right), Mainer's Mountaineers (bottom).

Billy in the Lowground

This tune will give you a feel for the relative minor sound. The sequence in this version is as follows:

1. Verse
2. 1st Chorus
3. Verse (repetition of verse played previously)
4. 2nd Chorus
5. Ending

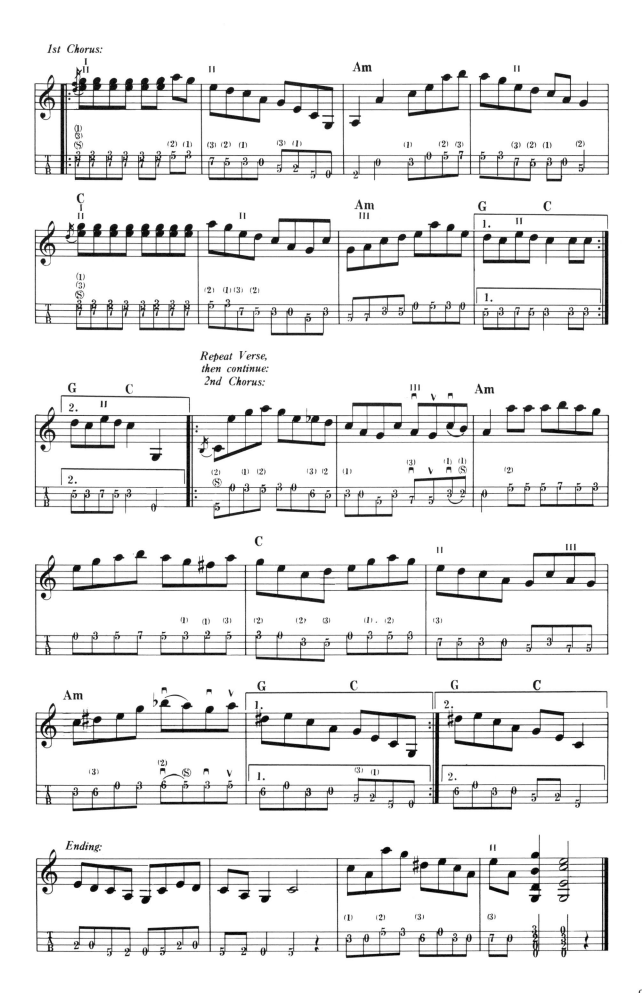

91

Blackberry Blossom

The verses in this tune are major, but the chorus is mostly minor. The fourth finger is used extensively, and the chords change twice per measure throughout most of the verse.

The second verse is a variation on the melody that works best when heard against the rapidly changing chords played on an accompanying instrument.

The sequence is:
1. 1st Verse
2. Chorus
3. 2nd Verse
4. Chorus
5. Ending

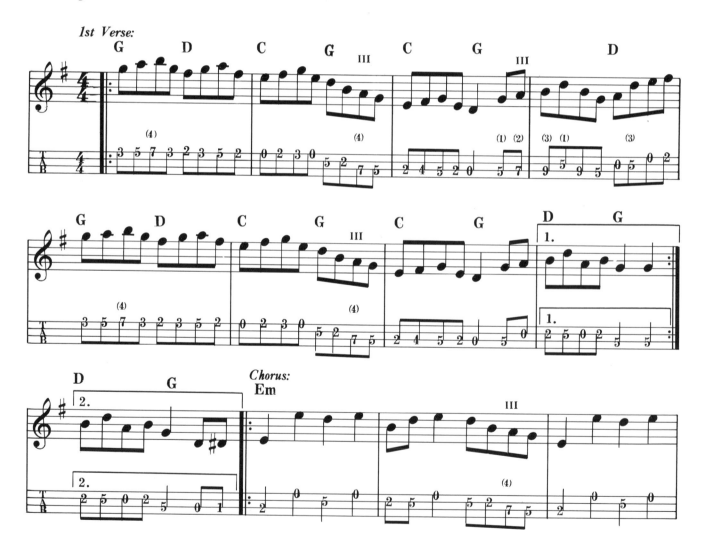

92

2nd Verse:

Repeat chorus; then play ending.

Ending:

Count: 1 & 2 & 3 & 4 &

The McReynolds roll or crosspicking style

Jesse McReynolds' mandolin roll style, or crosspicking as it has more recently been labelled, takes certain ideas from bluegrass banjo technique and applies them to the mandolin. Banjo players use three fingers (actually, the thumb plus the index and middle finger) to produce ringing phrases based on three different strings played in rapid succession. In crosspicking the same idea is applied to the mandolin. Instead of three individual fingers, however, the mandolin player must work with a single flat pick.

The most basic form of crosspicking consists of a series of eighth notes played as follows:

1. 3rd string   ⟨ *downstroke*
2. 1st string   *upstroke*
3. 2nd string   *upstroke*

Play this sequence over and over slowly on open strings. Make sure that there are no pauses between repetitions. You are now playing the pattern written below:

Notice that although the pattern you are playing is absolutely regular, you don't finish the pattern at the end of each measure. The reason is simple: A measure contains 8 eighth notes; you are playing a 3-note phrase. As 8 is not evenly divisible by 3, you will frequently have 1 or 2 notes left over which form the beginning of the next measure.

This fact can be used to add musical interest at times. At other times it is desirable to make the crosspicking phrases correspond exactly with the size of a measure. The simplest way to do this is to take the first measure of the above example and repeat it over and over:

We now have a *down-up-up-down-up-up-down-up* pattern, just one measure long.

Here is a straightforward exercise using roll number 2 all the way through. Be sure you never pause, even when you have to move the fingers of your left hand to a new position*

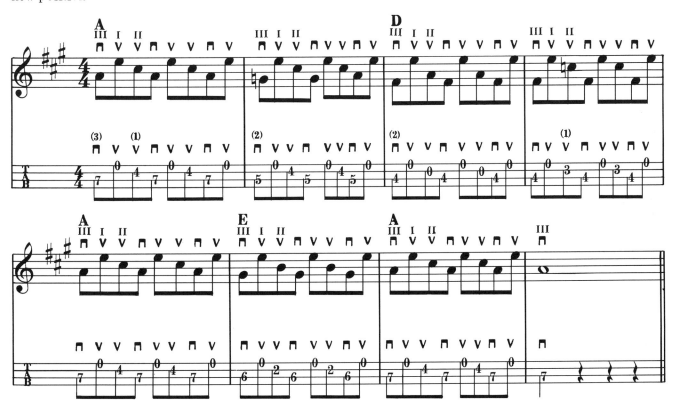

*if, in measure 3, the 1st string sounds a little strange to you, it is because an *e* note is not part of a D chord. In crosspicking, however, the open *e* string is played against various chords of which it is not part, and sounds fine when the passage is played up to the proper speed.

The next exercise contains both roll 1 and roll 2, and it will help to look in advance at how it is constructed:

1. Measures 1 through 3. All are roll 1. The fingers of your left hand change position at the end of each measure, but the roll (right hand picking sequence) continues unbroken.

2. Measure 4 and 5. These use roll 2.

3. Measure 6. Roll 1 finishes on the first note of the following measure.

4. Measures 7 and 8. Notice that the first note of measure 7 is a quarter note, which means a pause in the roll sequence. The next two repetitions of roll 1 are preceded by an upstroke on the 2nd string. Follow the count written under the tablature and you'll find the ending very satisfying.

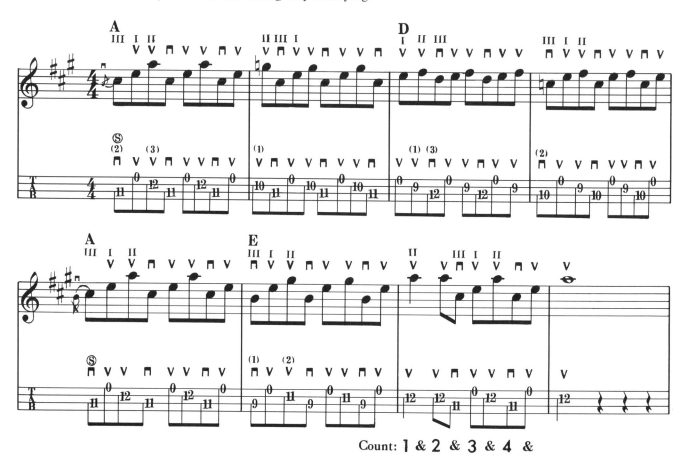

Count: **1 & 2 & 3 & 4 &**

When you can do the above exercises evenly and at a reasonable speed, try the following version of *Home Sweet Home.*

Notice that in places the roll is done on the three lowest strings (starting on the 4th) instead of the three highest. By far the greatest portion of the tune is based on roll 2.

Measures 28 and 29, however, use roll 1. (The dotted line in the measure is just to point out where the roll from the previous measure ends—it does not affect the timing.) In measures 5, 13, 16 and 32 the timing corresponds to measure 7 in the preceding exercise. And in certain places—measures 1, 9, and the end of 17—the roll is not employed.

Get into the tune easily, a few measures at a time. Until you can play it smoothly at a moderate tempo you may have trouble hearing it as music, but if your timing is good, it won't be long before it sounds impressive.

Home Sweet Home

Harmonics

One of the fascinating laws of physics that govern the behavior of musical instruments is that a picked string doesn't just vibrate from end to end (from bridge to nut). It also vibrates in halves.

String vibrating from end to end.

String vibrating in halves.

These two types of vibration produce two different notes. The note produced by the end-to-end vibration is much louder, so when we play the string open, we are only aware of the one note.

To hear the second, quieter, note, place your finger lightly on your 2nd string directly *over* the 12th fret (not behind the 12th fret where you would normally note it). Don't press down hard against the string, just let your fingertip feel the tiniest contact with it.

Now, play a single downstroke with your pick as you normally would. You should hear a bell-like ringing note, slightly quieter than your normal note. If you just get a

percussive thud with the pick, move the finger of your left hand slightly up or down the neck until you find the responsive place on your string. When you find it, you will be exactly halfway between the bridge and the nut.

The note produced on the 2nd string will be the next *a* note above the note produced by the open string, and should be the same pitch as the 12th fret of the string noted in the usual manner, even though the sound quality is different.

(There are additional harmonics as well at the 7th and 5th frets, and elsewhere. These, however, are so quiet as to be rarely, if ever, used.)

The next tune is a bluegrass adaptation of an old 19th century parlor tune, *Grandfather's Clock*. One short section uses harmonics (see box) so try your hand at them before getting into the tune.

Since most of the measures use roll 2, pick direction is not shown, except where it varies from this basic pattern. A number of measures (like measures 6 and 14) are very closely related to this pattern with a *down-up-down-up-up-down-up-up* sequence that takes up exactly one measure.

Roll 1 is used in passing from measure 22 to 23 and from measure 24 to 25. In this latter transition, your left hand shifts to a new position at the end of measure 24 even though you are still in the middle of the roll.

Be careful to stay with the count as written in measures 26 and 27. (Measures 34 and 35 are identical to these.) Also make sure you play the repeat as shown in the bridge.

Grandfather's Clock

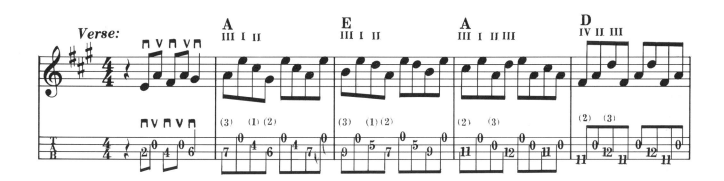

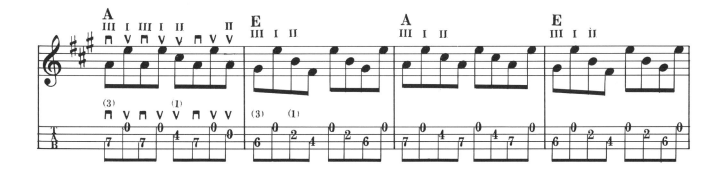

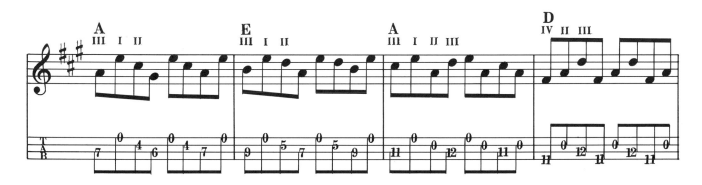

Chorus:

Count: 1&2 & 3 & 4 & 1&2 & 3 & 4 &

*Accompaniment plays a single brush downward on the first beat of the measure only.

Wildwood Flower

As mentioned earlier, this has long been a favorite for guitar pickers. Most of them play it in C, but they can easily move the capo up to the 2nd fret (where C position becomes D) and trade off breaks with the mandolin.

A new concept comes up briefly in this one, and it will come up again later. Up to now, each roll on the three highest strings has involved hitting the 3rd string as a downstroke and the 1st and 2nd strings as upstrokes. In the middle of measure 10, below, however, we have a roll consisting of:

1. 2nd string, 5th fret as a downstroke
2. 1st string, open, as an upstroke
3. 2nd string, 5th fret as an upstroke

Thus, it is possible to have a three-note sequence on just two strings, with the same pick direction as normally used on three different strings.

The same idea is used in measure 15 (and in measure 20 which is identical to it). In these measures also the 2nd string is hit both first and last in one roll. In these cases, though, a different fret is being noted the second time it is picked.

One last item: Starting at measure 23 there is a series of rolls (the roll 1 pattern) with a left hand position change after the open 1st string is played. The dotted lines dividing the measures make it easy to see where these changes occur. As you hit your 1st string each time, move your fingers to the next position.

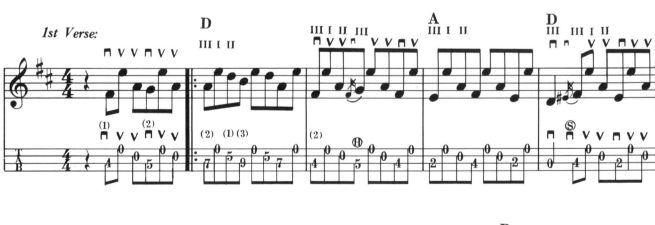

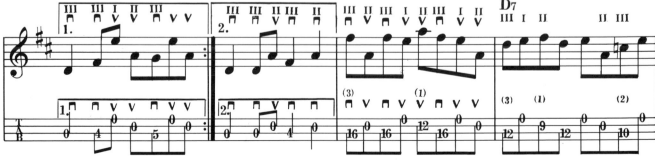

Black Diamond

Black Diamond is a banjo tune by Don Stover with some unusual and appealing chord changes.

For the end of measure 7 of this mandolin arrangement try holding both 2nd and 3rd strings at the 2nd fret, leaving the 1st string open. If it's hard to get both to come out cleanly, shifting the emphasis from 2nd to 3rd string may do the trick. Otherwise, use two different fingers to hold down these two strings.

Watch your pick direction, especially in the final eight measures, as there are a couple of slight variations on the patterns we've used so far.

Don Stover

Slickville

(Twin River Rag)

Slickville has a chord pattern similar to one used often in ragtime music and sometimes in bluegrass as well. It utilizes the same picking patterns we've done up to this point, but you'll find some new sounds stemming from the way they're used.

The introduction is played only once in the tune, at the beginning of the first verse.

Jack Tottle

* **The accompaniment plays only on the first beat of this measure and begins again with the next D7 chord.**

** **For the C#dim (C# diminished) chords use either of the following positions:**

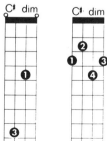

Variation 1.

* The accompaniment plays only the first beat of this measure and begins again with the next D7 chord.

Variation 2.

Count: 1 & 2 & 3 & 4 &

* The accompaniment plays only the first beat of this measure and begins with the next D7 chord.

Bill Monroe and the mandolin

There was a time—only as far back as the 1940's—when there was nothing called bluegrass music. There was, however, a popular Grand Ole Opry act called Bill Monroe and his Blue Grass Boys that sounded different from anything else in country music. So powerful was the appeal of the Monroe sound that before long other groups began forming along similar lines. As time passed they needed a word to describe what they were playing and "bluegrass music" came into the language.

Monroe's new music was a highly-charged blend of white music and black music. The prominence of the fiddle in bluegrass came from the white mountain music Bill learned from his uncle Pen Vandiver. The blues notes and syncopations were out of the blues tradition which Bill absorbed from black guitarist Arnold Schultz. In addition, his earliest church-going days taught Bill the power of strong vocal harmony.

His mandolin had attracted considerable attention well before Bill formed the Blue Grass Boys. In the late 1930's Bill and Charlie Monroe performed as a guitar and mandolin duet and recorded extensively for the RCA Bluebird label. Even then Bill's speed and dexterity set him apart from the relatively tame mandolin accompaniment prevalent in those rare instances when the instrument was used.

In the context of the Blue Grass Boys, however, Bill radically expanded the mandolin's role. With the action of the mandolin raised to facilitate loud, crisp chording, Bill used the instrument to control the band's rhythm. So distinctive and powerful was his offbeat chording that musicians swore he played "a different time" of his own.

As a lead instrument, Bill's mandolin exhibited a versatility without parallel in the playing of that time. His sweet smooth tremolo was flawlessly clean and even. His melodic backup was tasteful and interesting. While he could still play amazingly fast and smooth, as on the earlier Monroe Brothers recordings, Bill's breaks began to feature unique syncopations which would provide aggressive punctuation to the flow of a song. He also began using blues notes, and fashioned numerous phrases so effective that they later became integral parts of bluegrass mandolin playing.

In Bill's hands the mandolin evolved from a pretty and somewhat fragile instrument into one which could express a wide range of feeling, from a quiet moan to a menacing bark. Together with his keen sense of dynamics, this capability permitted dramatic mood changes within a given tune, which Bill used with stunning effect.

He also originated the bluegrass mandolin tune and composed a variety of types. Some, like *Blue Grass Stomp* and *Blue Grass Part One* were bouncy and at the same time bluesy. Others like *Bluegrass Breakdown* and *Rawhide* were fast, hard-driving and flashy. He also wrote a great many tunes for one or two fiddles, like *Roanoke* and *Scotland,* on which the mandolin plays an important part.

Bill's contributions to bluegrass by no means ended with his mandolin work. He experimented with a variety of vocal and instrumental combinations. He wrote many of the songs, like *Blue Moon of Kentucky* and *Uncle Pen* which have come to be integral parts of the bluegrass repertoire. And, of course, his characteristic high tenor voice has been imitated by countless bluegrass singers.

Over the years generations of the best bluegrass musicians have played with the Blue Grass Boys. Each of them learned from the experience, but each also contributed something of his own. Many of the earlier Monroe alumni, including Earl Scruggs, Lester Flatt, Don Reno, Jimmy Martin, Sonny Osborne, Carter Stanley, Don Stover, and Mac Wiseman went on to form bands of their own. More recent well-known graduates include Richard Greene, Del McCoury, Gene Lowinger, Pete Rowan, Roland White, Vic Jordan, Lamar Grier, Bill Keith and Byron Berline.

Part of Bill's genius as a band leader has been to sense how to develop and how best to utilize the abilities of these, and many other, excellent musicians. As his recordings testify Bill's various bands have, over the course of his career, produced an astonishing amount of exciting and inspired music.

Bill Monroe has been a focal point for bluegrass enthusiasts for several decades now. In the process he has attracted a considerable circle of admirers who view his style of music as the one *right* way to play bluegrass. Bill himself is more open-minded. As he sees it, "Every man that's played bluegrass has added something to it." He also points out that his own playing has undergone several major changes as well as a gradual evolutionary process year by year. "Bluegrass is different from what it was in the early days," he reflects. "There's more jazz in it now."

Although he doesn't analyze his music in elaborate detail, Bill has definite ideas about playing. "Some mandolin players don't get the best tone," in his view, "because they don't let the notes ring enough." He also stresses the importance of direct and uncluttered playing by noting, "Some people try to put too much into their music."

Much of Bill's work has, fortunately, been preserved on a large number of recordings. Some of the, best though by no means all, is included on the following albums: *The*

Original Sound (Harmony 7338), *Bill Monroe's Best* (Harmony HL 7315), *Bluegrass Instrumentals* (Decca 4601), *I Saw the Light,* (Decca DL 8769) *Blue Grass Style* (Vocalion VL 73870), *A Voice From On High* (Decca 75135), *The High Lonesome Sound* (DL 74780) *Country Music Hall of Fame* (Decca DL 75281) and *Mr. Blue Grass* (Decca DL 4080).

Bill's mandolin break on the traditional *Lonesome Road Blues* is a good example of how he plays a fast song. In some phrases the same note (or, where double strings are played, the same pair of notes) is played throughout. Sometimes, as in measures 1-4, a syncopated rhythm is used to add excitement.

Other, flashier, passages (like measures 9-15) require intricate left hand fingering. Bill is a master at using the contrast between the two approaches to draw enthusiastic applause from any audience.

Blue Grass Part One is typical of the medium tempo blues which Bill brought to bluegrass. Similar musical ideas are found in other Monroe instrumentals and in many of his mandolin breaks on medium tempo songs.

Both *Lonesome Road Blues* and *Blue Grass Part One* are from the Decca album, *Mr. Blue Grass.*

Blue Grass Part One contains a couple of items not treated previously:
Sixteenth notes. In certain instances two notes are played in the space normally occupied by a single eighth note. These are called sixteenth notes. A pair of sixteenth notes in tablature is written as:

Pulling off. Pulling off PO is the opposite of hammering on.
Note the 2nd string, 1st fret with your first finger and the same string, 3rd fret with your second finger. Pick the string. Immediately afterward *pluck* the string with the second finger of your left hand, pulling it sideways across the fingerboard. (The first finger remains in place.)
As with hammering on, two different notes are produced with a single pick stroke.

Charlie and Bill Monroe.

Lonesome Road Blues

Willie Broonzy

I'm goin' down this road feelin' bad,
I'm goin' down this road feelin' bad,
I'm goin' down this road feelin' bad Lord, Lord,
And I ain't-a gonna be treated this-a way.

I'm way down in jail on my knees, Lord, Lord,
I'm way down in jail on my knees,
I'm way down in jail on my knees Lord, Lord,
And I ain't-a gonna be treated this-a way.

They feed me on cornbread and beans,
They feed me on cornbread and beans,
They feed me on cornbread and beans Lord, Lord,
And I ain't-a gonna be treated this-a way.

Break:

* Downslide from 5th fret.

Blue Grass Part One

Bill Monroe

Introduction

1st Verse

2nd Verse

**Note; Pulling- off (po)---is from 3rd fret to 1st, fret in this tune.

*Slide from 3rd fret.

Next to last verse

Last verse

Four bluegrass greats

Bluegrass mandolin exists as the rich and vibrant art it is today because a variety of gifted musicians have each seen and developed different potentialities in the instrument. While a large number of excellent players are currently active, many of them quite young and dynamic, there are a select few whose accomplishments and contributions over the years merit particular attention. Of the numerous mandolinists to enter bluegrass subsequent to Bill Monroe it would be difficult to find any more influential than the four men discussed in this chapter.

Bobby Osborne

Bobby Osborne is an amazing singer. His powerfully high, clear and effortless vocals have dominated the Osborne Brothers' sound since the 1950's. While many singers, including some of Bobby's fellow professionals, periodically attempt, red-faced and with jugular vein throbbing noticeably, to duplicate his more dramatic vocal feats, he is without equal in his particular vocal style. So impressive is his voice that Bobby's contributions to bluegrass mandolin are sometimes overlooked.

He started out playing fairly straight conventional mandolin. The early recordings of the Lonesome Pine Fiddlers and later with Jimmy Martin on which Bobby appears give hints of original thought, but it was on a subsequent series of small label instrumental extended play 45's with his brother Sonny that Bobby first fully demonstrated his new and personal mandolin style.*

Previously most bluegrass mandolin breaks had consisted of several down-up strokes on an important melody note followed by several more down-up strokes on another important melody note, etc. There would often be runs connecting each of these stationary notes—sometimes elaborate ones—but the breaks seemed to depend on returning to the safety and stability of repeated down-up strokes in a given position.

By contrast Bobby played entire breaks of down-up strokes in which each note was different from the note preceding it. Nowhere did he land on a note and remain there. At the same time he moved sharply away from the established practice of sticking close to the melody. His sparkling solos seemed to float away from contact with the melody and then back in highly unpredictable ways.

In the following years the Osborne Brothers loosed numerous innovations on the bluegrass world, and it sometimes seemed that the mandolin might get lost in the shuffle. First, they modified the standard practice of trio singing in which the lead or melody part is the middle voice, with the tenor harmony above and the baritone harmony below. The Osbornes featured Bobby's high lead as the top voice and introduced contrary motion (one voice remaining on the same note or moving to a higher note while the others move down—or vice versa) into their trios.

*Some of these cuts were later released on *The Early Recordings of Sonny Osborne-Vol. 1* (Gateway 31385).

In the 1960's the brothers began using such non-bluegrass instrumentation as electric guitar, drums, pedal steel and piano to back them on record, which started moving them into an unusual position somewhere between country and western music and bluegrass. Later they amplified the banjo, mandolin and acoustic guitar, which, along with electric bass and drums, they used for live performances. This moved them further away from conventional bluegrass and they began to appear frequently with top country and western performers.

In terms of commercial success, the Osborne Brothers' singular approach paid off handsomely. They became regular members of the Grand Ole Opry and have received numerous coveted awards including the Country Music Association's Vocal Group of the Year. Their hit single of *Rocky Top* was one of the few by a bluegrass band to make the C & W charts, and was promptly rerecorded by over forty other performers.

Despite the vocal emphasis of the Osbornes' music and the C & W emphasis of a substantial amount of their material, there are excellent mandolin introductions and breaks throughout the group's numerous albums. One album, *Bluegrass Instrumentals* (MGM E/SE 4090) is, as the name implies, wholly instrumental. Bobby's most ambitious mandolin tune to date is *Sure-Fire* from *Up This Hill and Down* (Decca DL 74767), recorded in the early 1960's. *Fastest Grass Alive* (MCA 374) includes his first new mandolin tunes since *Surefire,* of which *M.A. Special* is one.

Sure - fire

* Accompanying instruments stop for 5 measures

2nd Chorus

* Accompanying instruments stop for 5 measures

*Accompanying instruments stop for 6 measures

M.A. Special

Verse: A

Bobby Osborne

Chorus:

✱ **Hammering-on is from 3rd fret to 4th.**

Repeat measures 9 through 16, then play ending.

(Portions of the above text on Bobby Osborne are from "The Osborne Brothers: Breaking Ground" by Jack Tottle in *Muleskinner News* July 1973, Copyright 1973. Used by permission.)

Jesse McReynolds

The early 1950's were exciting years for bluegrass. Many of the bands which would later dominate the music were just taking hold, and each new bluegrass release seemed to have something fresh and exuberant to say. Such competition notwithstanding, a series of gospel songs on an obscure label by an unknown group called the Virginia Trio startled the bluegrass world, and mandolin players in particular.

The group wasn't even a full bluegrass band, just a guitar, bass and mandolin with silky smooth trio vocals. Impressive though the singing was, the mandolin was the ultimate knockout. A waterfall of clear and precise notes cascaded over the listener, each with the purity of a tiny chime. A subtle tension built and receded in the course of each mandolin break. It was different from any other mandolin playing, and from any other sound in bluegrass.

The mandolin player was Jesse McReynolds, singing with his brother Jim. Jesse thought of the playing as "just my own style—kind of like a banjo roll." No one would call it "crosspicking" until ten years later.

Subsequent recordings (under the name of Jim and Jesse and the Virginia Boys) reflected Jesse's additional mastery of conventional mandolin playing, from slow to superfast. He also invented a split-string technique which enables him to play three-part harmony leads on the first two pairs of strings (see box).

(Portions of the above appeared in "Jim and Jesse: The Grass is Greener in the Mountains" by Jack Tottle, *Muleskinner News,* March, 1974. Copyright 1974. Used by permission.)

Splitting Strings

If you want to check out the idea of split strings, the following diagrams will give you an idea about how it's done. (Any possible dislocation of your fourth finger is at your own risk.)

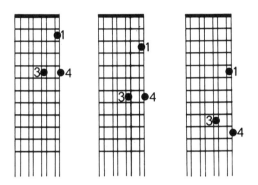

Eight strings, rather than the usual four are shown above since the outside string of the first pair, is noted individually. Both pairs of the 1st and 2nd strings are hit simultaneously. Try playing the three positions in sequence, then in reverse order.

Nevertheless, Jesse's mandolin roll retains the highest degree of fascination for bluegrass enthusiasts. Jesse freely admits that the idea for this style came from listening to some of Hoke Jenkins' banjo playing. (Hoke, a cousin of banjoist Snuffy Jenkins, played on Jim and Jesse's early Capitol recordings.) How on earth did Jesse ever conclude that it might be possible to move a flatpick in that strange pattern fast enough to work in an up-tempo song? "I just knew I could if I worked at it," he smiles.

Jesse thinks of the mandolin's first string as functioning like the banjo's fifth string—as a drone which is not noted and which remains constant through a song's various chord changes. One difference, however, is that on the banjo the fifth string is most often tuned to the key in which the song is played. For playing in G, the fifth string is tuned to a *g* note. When using the capo to play in A or B, the fifth string is brought up to *a* or *b* respectively.

On the mandolin, however, a capo is not used, and the 1st or *e* string is not retuned to correspond with the key of a given song. The repeating E note interacts with different chords in different ways and produces the building and receding of tension mentioned earlier.

Unlike most mandolin players, Jesse does not use a stiff pick. On live shows he uses a somewhat flexible plastic pick (medium); for recording he uses an even thinner pick and also lowers his strings, both of which undoubtedly contribute to his distinctive tone quality.

Over the years Jim and Jesse have recorded numerous excellent albums, some strictly bluegrass, others in a Country and Western vein. Among their best bluegrass albums are *Twenty Great Songs by Jim and Jesse* (Capitol DTBB-264), *Stars of the Grand Ole Opry* (with Flatt & Scruggs) (Starday SLP 365) *Ya'll Come* (Epic LN24144), and *Bluegrass Special* (Epic BN26031). *Mandolin Workshop* (Hilltop 202) has some good bluegrass and also some non-bluegrass mandolin arrangements.

Too Many Tears is from Jim and Jesse's great first sessions for Capitol recorded soon after the Virginia Trio material, and is included on the *Twenty Great Songs* album. *Stoney Creek* (from the *Bluegrass Special* album) was Jesse's first recorded roll style instrumental.

Too Many Tears

Jim McReynolds
Jesse McReynolds
Lucille Hutton

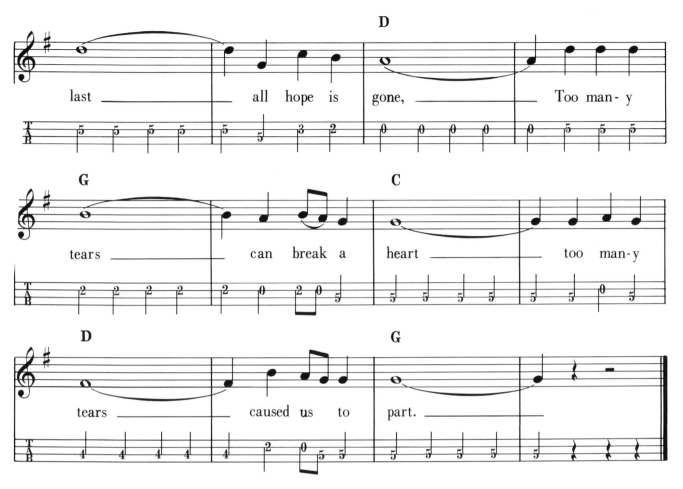

last _____ all hope is gone, _____ Too man-y

tears _____ can break a heart _____ too man-y

tears _____ caused us to part. _____

Too many times I've trusted you
Until you broke my heart in two
Too many tears has fell in vain
But now they've washed away the pain.

Each hour I've spent in lonely tears
You will regret in future years
There'll be no one to cry for you
Too many tears will make you blue

First Break

*Hammering on is from 7th fret.

Second Break

130

Stoney Creek

Jim McReynolds
Jesse McReynolds

Chorus:

Repeat Verse:

Frank Wakefield

One of the more colorful and controversial personalities in bluegrass as well as one of its foremost mandolinists, Frank Wakefield has long savored both roles with great relish.

It was in partnership with Red Allen during the latter 1950's and early 1960's that Frank first attracted widespread attention. Initially it was probably his uncanny ability to evoke both the aggressive drive and melodic content of Bill Monroe's style which stirred excitement among bluegrass enthusiasts. However before long it became apparent that using Monroe-style playing as a basis Frank could be quite creative on his own, and soon he had a loyal following who swore by his particular brand of hard-core bluegrass.

Most ear-catching was Frank's treatment of the blues notes. Monroe had most often used these in short, abrupt passages which tended to act almost as punctuation within a break. Frank integrated these same notes into longer melodic passages which stood out boldly from the major chords used to accompany them. (This is the same principle rock guitarists would discover a few years later and exploit so extensively.)

Frank also mastered playing in keys which were generally avoided by mandolin players. He would sometimes play through a tune once in G, then move it up one fret to G♯ for the second time around. The next time through he would move to A, then to B♭, and so on. His *New Camptown Races,* first recorded in the 1950's was the first important mandolin tune written in B♭, a key which most players of that time would have dismissed as too difficult to play in.

After recording with Red on a variety of labels including Folkways, Starday, Silver-Belle and Rebel, Frank joined the New York-based Greenbriar Boys. Whereas Frank and Red's partnership had resulted in a heavily rural flavored bluegrass sound, the Greenbriar Boys were all young city musicians. Different as their backgrounds were, Frank managed to fit in. Through the group's live performances and recordings on the Vanguard label *(Better Late Than Never,* VSD079233) Frank won increasing recognition from urban audiences.

In the mid 1960's the Greenbriar Boys disbanded and Frank began working independently. Performing frequently with a local band for backup, Frank would improvise much of the show depending on his mood and the capabilities of his accompanying musicians.

Frank enjoyed verbal improvisation as well. The evening he appeared on the same bill with Jimmy Martin for a concert in Cambridge, Massachusetts was typical. Jimmy had just opened his set with a fiery rendition of a Martin standard called *Sophronie.* As the enthusiastic applause died away the audience, most of whom had never seen Jimmy Martin before in person—waited in rapt silence. As Jimmy prepared to speak, Frank's voice from the wings boomed through the concert hall, "Hey, Jimmy! Play *Sophronie!*"

During this period Frank recorded an excellent album for Rounder Records (*Frank Wakefield,* 0007) backed by Country Cooking, which contains some excellent bluegrass mandolin and also some of Frank's original "classical" style on which he plays the mandolin unaccompanied. He also performed and/or recorded with Oliver, the New Riders of the Purple Sage and Don McLean.

Frank's best known instrumental is *New Camptown Races,* and it typifies his gutsy approach to Monroe-style playing. *Catnip* employs the minor passages referred to above. It also uses major notes on the low strings, the combination of which gives the tune an unusual and elusive feel. Both tunes appear on *Red Allen and Frank Wakefield* (Folkways FA2408).

New Camptown Races

Guitar: Capo at 3rd Fret.

Frank Wakefield

Catnip

Frank Wakefield

*From 2nd fret.

Repeat verse. Play chorus once more (without repeat), then continue:

∗ From 2nd Fret.

John Duffey

The son of a Metropolitan Opera singer, John Duffey turned down a chance to study music at the Peabody Institute near Baltimore, Maryland because he couldn't see how it could help him with bluegrass. Instead, he helped found one of the most innovative and, in its early years, underappreciated, bands in bluegrass, the Country Gentlemen.

In 1957 when John, Charlie Waller and Bill Emerson decided to call themselves the Country Gentlemen, bluegrass was a totally rural music. The material which was not strictly traditional showed a strong rural influence and nearly all the major performers were from the rural south.

The music was also rather deliberate. While some established groups had occasional comic relief, the overall approach to bluegrass was unrelentingly serious. City people on hearing bluegrass for the first time were struck by the paradox of a happy, sparkling music played by stoney-faced men in sombre grey suits.

John and his fellow Country Gentlemen joyfully broke all the rules. Spontaneously clowning on stage, climbing up on the railing around the bandstand, playing their instruments behind their heads and bellowing above the din or a noisy barroom crowd to "either shut up and listen or go down the street and yell someplace else" the group quickly attracted a sizeable following in the Washington, D.C. area. While retaining some standard bluegrass material, the Country Gentlemen thoroughly confused and disillusioned the hard core traditionalists by recording urban "folkie" material like *Copper Kettle,* Bob Dylan's *Baby Blue* and assorted other non-bluegrass material. Included in their repertoire were the movie theme *Exodus,* a jam on *The World is Waiting For the Sunrise* in which the melody is never suggested, much less actually played and *Big Bruce,* a spoof of Jimmy Dean's hit C & W recitation, *Big John.*

John Duffey's mandolin playing was just as irreverent. While most mandolin players of that time insisted firmly on playing the melody of the tune, punctuated by an occasional hot lick, John's approach seemed to be just the opposite. Gazing in apparent amazement at the antics of his fingers as they raced over the fingerboard, John would charge into a break crammed absolutely full of unlikely musical ideas. Frequently ending with a vicious chordal chop, John would stare defiantly at the audience as though daring anyone who had not been totally overwhelmed to speak right up.

Though he speaks admiringly of several important mandolin players who preceded him, John showed a clear preference for the untried over the playing styles which had already been proven successful. He choked his mandolin strings as a banjo picker or electric guitarist might; he used modern chords; he tried out using fingerpicks, one time along the lines of Jesse McReynolds' flatpick roll, another time like a Merle Travis fingerpicked guitar style. John played certain breaks on three strings simultaneously, creating a solid wall of sound with a rapid tremolo; on others he played sparsely, leaving big gaps between notes and creating interest through suprising syncopation.

For perhaps ten years the Country Gentlemen were essentially in a class by themselves—a bluegrass band drawing heavily on non-bluegrass material and playing techniques. Much of this period was an uphill battle for the band. The standard tough fight for survival in the music world was made tougher still by resistance to the Gentlemen's innovations from certain of the more conservative bluegrass elements.

John stayed with the Country Gentlemen long enough to see abundant vindication of the group's music by an enthusiastic reception on the bluegrass festival circuit in the latter 1960's. Then, after a two-year hiatus from music, he returned to help form the Seldom Scene. The new group, composed of highly talented Washington-area musicians, embodies many of the innovative qualities with which John has always been associated.

The mandolin break for *The Girl Behind the Bar* (from *Folk Session Inside; The Country Gentlemen,* Mercury MG20858) typifies John's unorthodox approach to a traditional-type bluegrass song. The timing is, to say the least, unusual. *Mean Mother Blues* (from *The Seldom Scene, Act III,* Rebel SLP 1528) is more in the folk-ragtime vein, and lends itself readily to John's flamboyance.

(Portions of the above are from *Don't Wait For Them to Buy—Sell It! John Duffey and His Music"* by Jack Tottle. Copyright 1974 by *Bluegrass Unlimited,* Inc. Used by permission.)

Top left, Akira Otsuka of the Japanese group, Bluegrass Forty-Five, and subsequently of Cliff Walton's New Shades of Grass. The unusual mandolin he plays was designed and built by John Duffey. Top right, Roland White. Roland has performed with the Kentucky Colonels, Bill Monroe, Lester Flatt and most recently, with Country Gazette. Bottom, Jimmy Gadreau with Charlie Waller, as a member of the Country Gentlemen. Jimmy has worked with the II Generation and The Country Store.

The Girl Behind the Bar

Mandolin Introduction:

Carter Stanley

Vocal:

As I walked in a way-side tavern

The smell of drink was in the air,

I threw my mon ey on the coun-ter

This pret-ty maid was stan-din' there.

D Mandolin Break:

*Hammer from 2nd Fret

My thoughts they drifted so far from me
As I looked upon her lovely face
I knew she was my kind of woman
No one could ever take her place.

I said "When workin' hours are over
I would just love to see you home."
She said, "Young man, this is my pleasure."
And soon we found ourselves alone.

And then our arms went round each other
I felt a knife stick in her back
She turned and saw her lover running
And said his name was Barnum Jack.

She did not know her lover followed
She did not know he was around
Until the fatal death had struck her
And now she sleeps beneath the ground.

I sit alone tonight in prison
My thoughts are of the one so fair
That I met that night in the wayside tavern
When the smell of drink was in the air.

Mean Mother Blues

Guitar: Capo at 5th Fret

John Starling

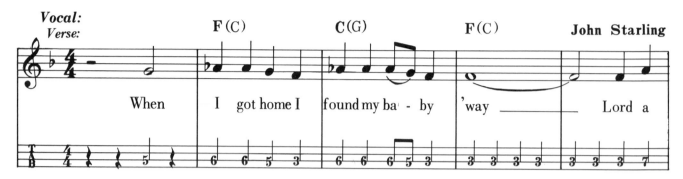

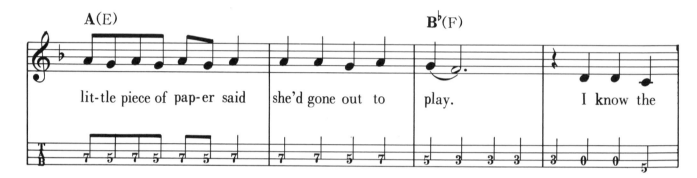

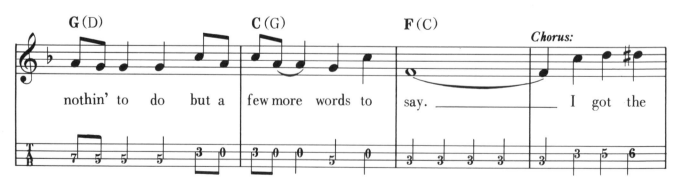

When she moved in I kissed the blues goodbye
She lit my torch then left the burners on high
Lord the money that I paid for that live-in lovin' maid
Now she's left me here to grieve moan and cry.

When you hear me singing you'll know just what I mean
Well I think it's all a part of a woman's scheme
If you're buying what she sells, she'll run you straight to hell
Captivate your mind and pick your trousseau clean.

Guitar: Capo at 5th Fret

* Ⓑ = Bend. The string is pushed across the fingerboard by the 3rd finger. This produces a twangy "bend" causing the original note to go sharp.

** Tremolo while sliding the 3rd finger from the 8th fret to the 10th.

Jethro Burns. For many years a member of the Homer and Jethro team, he has recorded in a bluegrass context with Wade Ray and The Country Fiddlers.

Gene Johnson with Wendy Thatcher of the II Generation.

Appendices

APPENDIX I
BUYING A MANDOLIN

A reasonably good instrument represents a sizeable investment for most of us. In buying, and to a certain extent, in caring for a mandolin it is helpful to have unbiased advice from someone who knows instruments. As it is not always easy to find a source who is both knowledgeable and impartial, the information and suggestions in this appendix may prove useful.

What kind of mandolin to buy? When you start shopping around you will find that mandolins may be round-backed, flat-backed or arch-backed. Some mandolins have round sound holes; others have f-shaped holes. Many are teardrop shaped, but others have points or scrolls protruding from them.

From the standpoint of the mandolin as a bluegrass instrument, the following categories can be useful in determining what kind of mandolin is the best buy.

Round-back
mandolin.

1. Round-back mandolin: Also called a bowl-back or tater bug, the best of the round-back mandolins have a sweet delicate sound. They were extremely popular in the 19th century America, and a surprising number of fairly old ones are still to be found, Despite the difference in appearance from the mandolins professional bluegrass musicians use, a good round-back is quite satisfactory for learning fundamentals should you already have one. In playing with other bluegrass instruments, however, you will find that the louder instruments such as steel-strung guitar, banjo and fiddle will tend to overpower the round-back mandolin.

Pre-war Stradolin.

2. Miscellaneous flat-back or arch-back mandolins: Mandolins with flat or gently-arched backs are more recent inventions, though some were made as early as the 1800's. Among the best-made of these are those by Vega, Washburn, Weymann, Lyon and Healey, and Martin. (Of these companies, only Martin presently manufactures mandolins, and the craftsmanship continues to be excellent.) There are also in existence a number of pre-World War II mandolins made by Harmony, Stella and Stradolin which are quite good.

The above-mentioned mandolins, along with other makes using the same basic design tend to be better for bluegrass as they can be played more aggressively than the roundbacks. Their tone is less fragile and their ability to project sound when played with other instruments is greater.

3. Gibson mandolins: With very few exceptions, professional performers use Gibson mandolins. The old F-5 models favored by the majority of professionals are quite expensive and hard to locate, but a number of the less costly models made since the turn of the century can still be found.

Gibson A-4 mandolin.

The most common models of the teardrop-shaped round-hole series (the soundhole is actually oval) are the A Jr., A-0, A-1, A-2, A-3 and A-4. These are all of essentially the same design, with varying finishes, types of wood, and amounts of ornamentation. Models A-40 and A-50 are also constructed along similar lines, but these have f-holes instead of the oval sound hole.

Gibson F-5 mandolin, made by Lloyd Loar, the creator of the F-5 design.

The other major category is the artist model series. Mandolins of this series have a scroll and points which alter the basic Gibson teardrop shape. Some, like the F-2 and F-4 have the oval soundhole; others, like the F-7, F-12 and F-5 have f-holes.

Generalizations about the relative merits of different mandolin models can't be taken as absolute rules. There may be great variation in sound between two mandolins of the same model made in the same year. However, the Gibson A-series mandolins do tend to have superior volume and tonal characteristics for bluegrass over the other types of mandolins discussed earlier. Similarly, the F-series mandolins tend to be better than the A-series in these qualities. Nevertheless, F-series mandolins are priced very much higher, and for the non-professional, an A-series mandolin is often a more sensible buy.

Where to look: New mandolins can be purchased through regular music stores. You can quickly find out what is available by a few phone calls to local dealers. In purchasing a new mandolin you also have the advantage of buying from an established businessman who, presumably, has a stake in backing the product he sells. (Even on new instruments different stores may sell identical items at different prices, so shop around as much as you can.)

Used mandolins are also worth considering, for several reasons. Not only are older mandolins usually less expensive than similar new models, but quality of materials and workmanship is better in a great many of the mandolins made prior to World War II. This has a direct bearing not only on appearance and feel but on sound quality as well.

Unlikely as it may seem, a good instrument also improves with age as it is played. Mandolins found stored in attics for thirty years don't sound nearly as good as equivalent instruments which have been in constant use. (The process has not been precisely analyzed, but it seems to be the cumulative effect of the vibrations which playing sends through the instrument.)

The availability of good used instruments depends on where you are located. Many regular music stores sell new instruments almost exclusively. A store which deals primarily in acoustic folk instruments is more likely to have or know of a used mandolin for sale than a store which sells primarily electric guitars, amplifiers and drums. Other leads on a good used mandolin might come from local music teachers, instrument repairmen or bluegrass performers. Pawnshops and local want ads are also possibilities. If you have the opportunity to attend a bluegrass festival, you can keep your eye out for instruments for sale, and also ask around during the parking lot jam sessions.

What to look for in a mandolin: As with buying anything in used condition, it is most ideal if you can buy from someone in whom you have confidence. The chances are, of course, that when you do finally run down a prospect it won't be your bosom buddy from childhood hawking a mint condition pre-war gem on the corner. You should, therefore, be prepared to check a few basic items yourself.

Before you start, the instrument should be fully strung up and tuned to standard pitch. Then take a look at the following:

1. Action. The *action* depends on the distance between the strings and the fingerboard. If the action is too low, the strings will buzz when played at certain frets. If it is too high, the strings will be hard to press down against the fingerboard.

Many mandolins have adjustable bridges, and those that don't can have their bridges raised or lowered easily by a repairman. The nut can likewise be adjusted should it be necessary. Until the action is reasonably correct, however, you can't get a real idea of how the mandolin will play or sound.

2. Neck. Sighting down the fingerboard, the neck should be seen to be pretty straight. If the tension of the strings has pulled the neck sufficiently to bow it forward, you will probably have high action up around the 12th fret, buzzing of the strings at certain frets, or a problem with some notes sounding off pitch.

Another way to check the neck is by pressing down one string at a time at the 12th or 14th fret. Look at the portion of the string between that fret and the *nut*. If it does not lie quite close to the intervening frets, the neck is bowed.

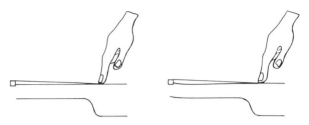

Some mandolins have an adjustable steel rod in the neck, which can be tightened by a repairman to correct this condition. On mandolins without the adjustable neck rod straightening a bowed neck is likely to be expensive.

3. Cracks, scratches, and separating seams. Minor cracks can usually be patched without difficulty by a repairman and without hurting an instrument's tone. Scratches in the finish are to be expected on an older instrument, though if they are excessive they will, naturally, reduce its value. (Refinishing is pretty expensive, and an amateur job can be disastrous both to tone and appearance.)

If a seam has come unglued, for example between the sides and back, this can normally be reglued provided that the wood has not warped in such a way that the parts no longer match.

4. Intonation. *Intonation* describes how closely the notes produced by an instrument approximate their correct pitch. Poor intonation means that even though an instrument's strings are tuned properly, certain notes played on them sound noticeably sharp or flat. Good intonation means that all notes sound as they should. If the neck is straight the intonation of any sound, well-made instrument will be fine. Should an adjustment in intonation be necessary, the bridge can be moved slightly, which any repariman or music teacher can readily do. You can even do it yourself, as described below.

Intonation and bridge placement
One way of checking the intonation is by playing the 12th fret harmonic of each string as described on page 98. As mentioned, the 12th fret harmonic should be the same pitch as the note played normally at the 12th fret.

If these do not correspond on each string, it may just mean that the bridge is not where it should be, i.e. exactly as far from the 12th fret as the 12th fret is from the nut.

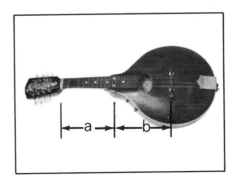

If the normal note is higher in pitch than the corresponding harmonic, the bridge should be moved very slightly toward the tailpiece. (To move the bridge, loosen the strings a little-the bridge should never be held in place by glue—and slide it into position.) If the normal note is lower in pitch than the harmonic, the bridge should be moved toward the fingerboard.

Once the notes and the harmonics match on all strings (you'll need to bring any string you check back up to standard pitch) the intonation should be right. This can be double checked by playing notes and chords at various points on the neck to confirm that no sour notes occur.

5. Tone and volume. Given that an instrument is basically sound and playable, its most important qualities are tone and volume.

When you first begin learning the mandolin you may feel that just finding where your fingers are supposed to go and synchronizing your right hand with your left takes all your attention. Tonal quality may seem like the least of your concerns. After awhile, however, you will inevitably begin listening to the sounds you produce. The better your instrument, the better you'll sound and the more you'll enjoy playing.

APPENDIX II
GETTING THE MOST FROM YOUR INSTRUMENT

Owning a mandolin is much less trouble than owning, let's say, a chicken, or even a car. To get the most out of your investment, though, it is helpful to bear in mind a few items of background information.

General Care: A good mandolin will last a lifetime and more with very little special attention. The following points relating to care, are, however, important:

1. *The case:* A good instrument deserves a good sturdy case. A cardboard case makes sense for a relatively inexpensive mandolin; it will keep off a light sprinkle of rain and prevent scratches. However, an expensive instrument should have a sturdy hardshell case, usually made of laminated plywood covered with fabric or imitation leather.

2. *Temperature/humidity:* Unnecessary extremes of heat, cold, wetness and dryness should be avoided. This just means don't leave your mandolin locked in a car trunk for prolonged periods in cold weather or under a hot summer sun. Also, don't store it next to a hot radiator or heat duct at home.

3. *Shipping:* If you are ever forced to ship it, be sure your instrument is packed well, crated, the strings loosened to half tension and the end pin, if any, removed. (This last is to prevent the entire shock of being dropped from being centered at one point and breaking the instrument.) Don't fail to insure it enroute.

(Airlines are notorious for breaking musical instruments, but mandolins are small enough so that you may be able to carry yours as hand luggage if you take a plane trip.)

4. *Precautions against theft:* Mandolins, like other musical instruments are attractive items to steal. They are light, portable, and easily saleable. If you leave yours on the back seat of your car while parked in any city or sizeable town (even under a blanket or similar camouflage) there is a very good chance it won't be there when you return.

If you have an instrument that would be hard to replace record its serial number. This one step can mean the difference between recovery and loss in the event of theft. If there is the remotest chance your home or apartment might be broken into, keep your mandolin away, out of sight and preferably locked up when your not home. If you have household insurance, make sure the coverage extends to your mandolin; if not, you may find it worthwhile, depending on its appraised value, to insure it separately.

Getting the best sound from your mandolin. A stringed instrument produces sound as follows:

1. The pick strikes the strings causing them to vibrate.
2. The vibration of the strings causes the bridge to vibrate.
3. The vibration of the bridge causes the instrument, especially the top to vibrate.
4. The vibration of the instrument causes vibrations in the air, which are picked up by our ears as sound.

The wood used in the mandolin has a great deal to do with the sound it produces. So does the way the wood is assembled. There are, however, other variables over which you have some control:

1. *Thickness of strings.* The heavier the gauge of a string, the tighter it must be tuned to bring it up to standard pitch. The tighter it is tuned, the greater the tension on the bridge and the resultant pressure on the mandolin's top.

Gibson mandolins are made to withstand the pressure of a heavy gauge string, and Gibson strings, which are relatively heavy gauge, are probably the most popular with Gibson owners. These would, however, put disastrous tension on a lightly built mandolin which could cause the neck to bow forward or the top to collapse. There are various lighter weight strings available for the more lightly built mandolins.

(A lightweight string on a sturdily constructed mandolin won't, of course, hurt it. Tone and volume will be less than the instrument is capable of, though, because with the tension reduced the top will vibrate less when the string is picked.)

2. *Composition of the strings.* In some sets of mandolin strings, all are made of steel. In others, the wound strings are bronze and the exact composition of the metal used may vary among different makes. Which sounds best on a given mandolin depends on individual taste and the instrument involved. It is worth experimenting to find the string you like best.

3. *Type of bridge.* Some mandolins are made with solid, one-piece bridges. Others have adjustable bridges which are raised or lowered by means of two small wheels. The style, mass and composition of the bridge can have an effect on sound, though usually a fairly minimal one.

4. *Bridge height.* As noted earlier, for a mandolin to be playable, the bridge must hold the strings high enough off the fingerboard so that they don't buzz. It must also be low enough so you can readily press the strings against the frets.

However, as the bridge height increases, so does the tension on the top. With most mandolins, as this tension increases—so—within limits—does volume. The tone may also become more brilliant with increased bridge height.

As a result, many mandolin players raise their action quite high, even though this necessitates pressing down harder on the strings.

When you are starting out, there is no need to raise the action particularly high. However, as time passes, your fingers will gain in strength and you may find you like the sound of your mandolin with the action slightly higher.

Changing strings. About the only periodic maintenance you'll need to do is the changing of strings.

Strings begin to rust as soon as you start using them. Since moisture from your hands and, to some extent, moisture from the air hasten this process, your strings will last longer if you wipe them with a soft cloth after each use. Wipe them from the top, and also from underneath by passing the cloth between strings and fingerboard.

When sufficient rust has built up, the string will lose all traces of its original brilliance and tone. It will sound dull and thuddy.

With prolonged use, the wound strings will show signs of wear at the frets most often played. Eventually the winding will wear through, showing the plain steel wire underneath. When this happens, it is past time to change strings. (By this time the intonation of the strings will probably be slightly off due to unevenness where the strings are worn.)

Every two or three months is plenty often to change strings—some people wait much longer. You should, however, keep extra strings in your case in the event you should break one. When you are practicing by yourself you may not play hard enough to break strings, but once you start playing with other people, you may well find yourself bearing down hard enough to do so every so often. At any rate, there is nothing so frustrating as being all set for an evening of playing, whether with friends or at home alone, and suddenly finding you have a broken string with no replacement anywhere around.

When changing an entire set of strings, it is desireable to replace a couple of individual strings at a time, tune them up with the remaining six strings, then change another two, etc. until all have been replaced. This maintains a fairly constant tension on the mandolin and makes it much easier to get it into good tune with the new strings. (Even so, there will always be some slippage until the new strings are fully stretched out.)

Most mandolin strings have loop ends, which fit over small hooks on the tailpiece. (The tailpiece may have a cover which either pulls straight up or slides forward.)

At the headstock the strings are, of course, wound around the posts which are turned by means of the tuning keys.

Described below is a simple and secure way to thread the string which holds slippage to a minimum:

1. After hooking the loop end to the tailpiece, run the string straight through the hole in the corresponding post in the headstock. Leave a little play in the string, but not too much.

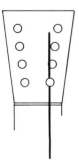

2. Bring the string around the post to the *inside* and *under* itself where it enters the post.

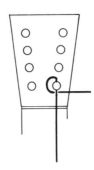

3. Bring the end of the string back around to the inside again, this time *over* itself where it enters the post.

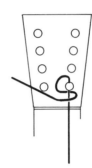

4. Keeping a gentle pressure on the string, so it doesn't come undone, turn the tuning key so that the string winds to the *inside* of the post. The string will be securely locked around itself, but will still be easy to remove when it is eventually replaced.

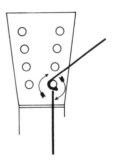

(Note: When tightening the string, guide it toward the lower portion of the post, so that it can't slip over the top. The play left in the string in Step 1 above should allow the string at least two turns around the post by the time it is brought up to pitch.)

APPENDIX III
TUNING: SOME ADDITIONAL POINTS
Staying in tune

In the course of playing the mandolin may, as mentioned elsewhere, get slightly out of tune. If one or more notes begin sounding a little sour, check carefully to see which string is wrong before tuning any string. Play the individual strings of each pair to see in which case the two are not identical notes. When you find a pair whose notes don't match, check the 7th fret of the next lower string to see which of the pair is incorrect. (It is, of course, also possible that both have gone out of tune.)

If you start tuning without checking all the strings you may end up retuning to a string which is itself not in tune. This will result in retuning the entire mandolin, which is a lot more work than just correcting one or two strings.

Tuning up vs. tuning down

Most musicians prefer to tune up to the correct note, rather than down. This means that even if the string being tuned is above (or sharp, to) the reference note, it is first brought down below (or flat, to) that note. Next, the reference note is sounded (whether on another instrument, a tuning fork, or another string of the mandolin). While it is still ringing, the tuning key is turned evenly to bring the string up in pitch until it is equal to that of the reference note.

Effects of changing tension

If you have to alter the pitch of the string more than a small amount to get the mandolin tuned, you are altering the tension on the instrument. As you tighten the strings, for example, the increased pressure forces the bridge a little harder against the top and causes the strings to pull harder against the neck. Solid though the instrument may seem, the top actually sinks slightly and the neck is pulled a little forward. Loosening the strings will, naturally, have the opposite effect.

Suppose that the mandolin is tuned substantially low and that you bring it up to the correct pitch by tuning first the 4th string, next the 3rd string, and so on until you finish with the 1st string. By the time the final string is tuned, changes in the top and neck will mean that even though the lower strings were correct when you tuned them, they are now below the proper pitch. You will thus need to go over all the strings again. Sometimes it is necessary to recheck the strings a couple of times before all stresses have been equalized.

Staying at, or slightly above, a standard pitch.

From the above paragraph, it is obvious why you don't want to alter the overall pitch of the instrument unnecessarily. You might wonder, however, why tuning to standard pitch (that of a tuning fork or piano) is preferable to any other range.

The mandolin is, like any instrument, designed for standard pitch. If you tune the strings much lower, the tension on the instrument is less. As a result, the top of the instrument vibrates less, and tone and volume are impaired.

If you tune far above standard pitch, you are creating more tension than the instrument is built for. You are more likely to break strings. The neck is more likely to warp or pull out from the body of the instrument and the top could buckle or crack under the stress.

For these reasons, performers generally play either at standard pitch or, to achieve a little more brilliance, just slightly above.

APPENDIX IV
THE RIGHT HAND: A DETAILED LOOK

There are quite a few things happening each time you pick a string with your right hand, and there is no way to concentrate on each one of them at once. If you feel your picking technique could stand some improvement, read through the following description and take one, or maybe two, ideas that differ from what you are doing. If a new idea helps, keep it. If not, discard it and try another.

The right hand is held in a loose fist, with the thumb on top of the index or first finger. The second, third, and fourth fingers are not tucked in tightly, but remain roughly in line with the first finger.

The pick is inserted between the thumb and first finger. The more flesh in contact with the pick, the less likely it is to slip, and the less pressure you need to keep it under control. The pick should be covered by the fleshy part of the first joint of the thumb, and should be supported by the first finger at approximately the first knuckle. (i.e. the knuckle nearest the nail.)

The first joint of the first finger is somewhere between parallel and a 45 degree angle with the thumb. It should not point inward, directly at the mandolin. (See picture below.)

The thumb should be approximately straight. If the thumb bends downward, the pick will be held by the end of the thumb, which has insufficient surface area. This can lead to overtensing the hand in an effort to keep the pick from slipping. A similar problem can occur if the pick is held too far back, under the knuckle of the thumb. In this case there is bone, with very little flesh, above the pick and thus a tendency for the pick to slip out of control.

Thumb bent downward.

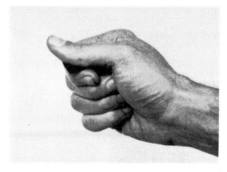

Pick under knuckle.

The pick should be held loosely. This is most important, especially at the beginning, since smooth up-and-down picking depends largely on this aspect. Don't be concerned that volume is lessened by the looseness. As time goes by you will learn how much you can tighten your grip without impairing your smoothness. For now, assume that if you drop the pick, you are holding it too loosely—otherwise you're not.

Some mandolin players (like John Duffey and Jesse McReynolds) rest the third and/or fourth fingers on the mandolin. Others (including Bill Monroe and Frank Wakefield) do not. Resting the fingers may give silghtly better control on intricate passages, but it also may interfere with tone.

In any event, the fingers of the right hand should never touch the mandolin when you accompany a voice or another instrument by playing chords. This would interfere with the necessary free, sharp stroke across all four strings.

The wrist is bent very slightly inward. When hitting the string with the pick, the impetus comes from the wrist just barely bent and without moving your forearm. (The forearm need not be totally rigid, but any movement should be only in response to the wrist's action.)

The reason for playing with a loose wrist instead of stiffening the wrist and letting the elbow do the work is the same as the reason you write holding a pencil near the point, rather than at the end near the eraser: A small, precise motion is most readily controlled close to the point of action, rather than at a distance.

The hand does not twist or dip, whether on a downstroke or an upstroke with the pick. The hand remains parallel to the face of the mandolin. Whatever "give" is required as the pick passes across the string (or strings) is accomplished by the looseness with which the pick is held.

Neither the index finger nor the thumb should move in relation to the rest of the hand. The path of the pick is controlled only by the action of the wrist.

The angle of the pick is quite important. It should be roughly perpendicular to the face of the mandolin. If slanted sharply upward to facilitate the downstroke, it will tend to catch on the string on the upstroke.

Pick slanted.

Pick straight.

The pick should also be parallel to the strings as it strikes them. While there is sometimes a tendency to turn the pick in order to glide over the strings more easily, this produces a considerable loss of tone and a highly undesireable pick noise.

Above all, try to stay relaxed. Don't tense muscles you don't need, such as your shoulder, upper arm or forearm. Don't press your arm tightly against your body, and don't force your elbow out, away from you. Try to eliminate any trace of conflict between yourself and the mandolin. Instead, think of working with the instrument to create the best sound possible.

APPENDIX V
THEORY LESSON

Music theory is a vast, complex and, if you have an aptitude for translating the abstract into the practical, a fascinating field.

There are, happily, a few simple ideas that can provide helpful insight into how bluegrass music is constructed. This chapter explains how you can tell the names of the notes you are playing, what a key is, which chords are most common in any given key, and how to **transpose** chords from one key to another.

Naming the notes. The names of the notes come from the first seven letters of the alphabet: **a, b, c, d, e, f, g.** In addition to these notes, called *naturals*, there are other notes which fall in between. These other notes can be expressed as *sharps* (♯) or *flats* (♭).

A sharped note is one fret higher than its natural counterpart. An *a*♯ note, for example, is one fret higher than an *a* note.

A flatted note is one fret lower than its natural counterpart. An *a*♭ note is one fret lower than an *a* note.

The entire sequence of notes including naturals, sharps and flats is as follows. It is called the chromatic scale.

Notice that just one note falls in the scale between the *a* note and the *b* note. This note can be called *a*♯ (one fret above *a*). It can also be called *b*♭ (one fret below *b*.)

The same pattern holds true between *c* and *d*, between *d* and *e* and so forth. A note which falls between two natural notes can be designated in terms of either a sharp or a flat.

The chromatic scale shown above encompasses all the notes between an *a* note and the next higher *a* note. This interval is called an *octave*.

The mandolin like other instruments is not limited to a single octave. It has, in fact, a range of three full octaves, which simply consist of the same sequence of notes repeated three times.

Full Range of the Mandolin:

Rather than try to memorize the location of each note on the fingerboard, just think of the scale as:

a, *a♯*, *b*, *c*, *c♯*, *d*, *d♯*, *e*, *f*, *f♯*, *g*, *g♯*

(You can always figure out the flats if you need them.)

Or, you can remember one simple rule: **Each natural note has a corresponding sharp with the exceptions of b and e.**

Knowing that your strings are tuned to *g*, *d*, *a*, and *e* you can readily find the name of any note you play. Starting with your open string, just count up one fret at a time.

For example: play your 4th string, 4th fret. Your 4th string is tuned to *g* open. The 1st fret is therefore *g♯*; the 2nd fret is *a*; the 3rd fret is *a♯* and the 4th fret is *b*. The same process works anywhere on the fingerboard.

Shifting chord positions around. The application of all this is most readily obvious with respect to chords. Once you know the chromatic scale, you can understand why the major chords you have learned fall as they do. And you can use the knowledge to form any major chord you need.

Moving the G chord up one fret results in a G♯ or A♭ chord. One fret higher, you have an A chord. Still another fret up gives you an A♯ or B♭ chord. And so forth, as high as you might want to go.

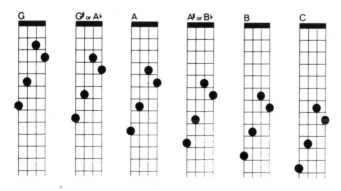

The same pattern holds when you move the C chord position up the neck, a fret at a time:

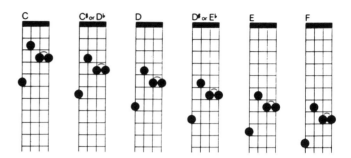

Key. The key of a song is determined by the most important note in that song. It is normally the last note of the melody, and nearly always accompanied by the chord having the same name.

If a bluegrass song ends on a *d* note, and is accompanied by a D chord, then it is in the key of D. If it ends with an *a* note along with an A chord, it's in the key of A. (In those unusual cases where the chord is different from the note, the chord will generally correspond with the key of the song.)

The idea of key is helpful in that it provides an idea of what chords we will play in accompanying any given song. The tunes we've done in the key of D (*Wildwood Flower, Soldier's Joy*) use D, G and A chords for accompaniment. Those in the key of A use either A and E chords (*Old Joe Clark*) or A, D and E (*Cripple Creek, Jesse James, Boil Em Cabbage Down*).

Finding the principal chords in an unfamiliar key can be difficult if you approach it by trial and error. There is, however, a simple device for discovering them. It is called the Circle of Fifths:

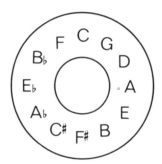

Circle of Fifths

The chord whose name corresponds to the key is called the *tonic*. (In the key of G, the G chord is the tonic.)

Find the tonic of the key you want to examine in the Circle of Fifths. Now move one step in a clockwise direction. This chord is the *dominant* for the key you are concerned with. The dominant generally occurs as the next to last chord of the tune (just before the final tonic chord), and, often, elsewhere in the tune in addition. (In the key of G, the dominant is D.)

Now go back to the tonic, and move one step in a counterclockwise direction. This brings you to the *subdominant*. If a song contains more than two chords the subdominant is most likely to be the third one. (In the key of G, C is the subdominant chord.)

Transposing from one key to another. Suppose you find a song in a songbook in the key of C. Instead of just the tonic, subdominant and dominant (C, F, and G) let's say it contains A and D chords as well as G and C.

Let's also assume that the key of C is a little low for you to sing this particular song and you want to do it higher, for example, in the key of D. How would you know what chords to use in the new key?

If you know the chromatic scale, it's very easy. Just lay out the chords of the song in its original key. Put the tonic of the new key under the tonic of the original.

Chords in the original key:	C	A	D	G
New key:	D			

Now, calculate how many notes you would have to move along the chromatic scale to get from the original tonic to the new one. In this case, referring to the chromatic scale on page 155 we find that, starting at C, we must go forward two notes (C♯ and D) to reach D.

Chords in the original key	C	A	D	G
Distance on the chromatic scale	+2			
New key	D			

Now, take the first chord you want to transpose to the new key, and, using it as your starting point on the chromatic scale, move the same distance. Two notes above A on the scale (A♯ and B) is B.

Chords in original key	C	A	D	G
Distance on chromatic scale	+2	+2		
New key	D	B		

Apply the same process to the remaining chords. This gives you:

Chords in original key	C	A	D	G
Distance on chromatic scale	+2	+2	+2	+2
New key	D	B	E	A

(Notice that as you move up 2 notes from G, you don't run out of notes at the end of the scale. You just move up into a new octave and start the scale over again: the first step up is G♯; the second is A.)

If you had wanted to transpose the same song to a lower key you might have moved it down to A. Since A is three notes *back* from C on the chromatic scale, your transposition would end up as follows:

Chords in original key	C	A	D	G
Distance on chromatic scale	-3	-3	-3	-3
New key	A	F♯	B	E

The same idea holds, regardless of the kinds of chords used, from any key to any other.

APPENDIX VI
READING MUSIC
A BRIEF WORD ON STANDARD MUSIC NOTATION

Unless you already read music you will probably use the tablature line for the tunes in this book. If you want to relate it to standard music notation, the following may be helpful.

The notes which correspond to the open strings of the mandolin are as follows:

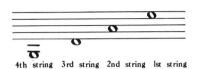

4th string 3rd string 2nd string 1st string

Time values. The duration, or time value of a note is indicated by its form. (Whether the stem points up or down does not affect how it is played.)

Whole note

Half note

Quarter note

Eighth note

Sixteenth note

Two or more eighth notes, and notes of smaller time value can be grouped together as follows:

A whole note lasts the same length of time as two half notes. Or, put another way, a half note goes by twice as fast as a whole note.

The pyramid below illustrates that the same time elapses for a single whole note, two half notes, four quarter notes, and so forth:

Another symbol for expressing time value is the *dotted note*. A note with a dot next to it has its normal duration increased by half again its value. A dotted half note, for example is a single note played with the same duration as a normal half note followed by a quarter note.

has the same duration as

has the same duration as

Rests. An interval of silence between notes is called a rest. Its duration is the same as the note which corresponds to it. Thus, a whole rest lasts as long as a whole note; a half rest as long as a half note, etc.

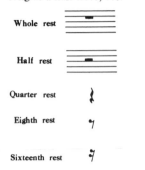

Whole rest

Half rest

Quarter rest

Eighth rest

Sixteenth rest

Key signature. Accidentals may be placed at the beginning of each line of music, immediately following the clef sign. These comprise the *key signature* and indicate that the notes to which they apply are to be altered throughout the piece.

All f's and c's are played as f#'s and c#'s respectively.

All b's are played as b♭'s

The effects of the key signature can be modified by use of additional accidental signs within the body of the piece. When used in this manner, the accidental signs are in force only in the measure in which they appear.

Ralph Rinzler, noted folklorist and former member of the Greenbriar Boys.

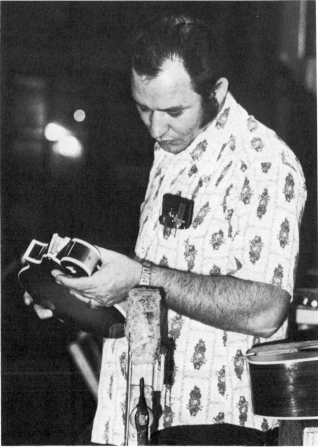

Randy Wood in his Nashville workshop.

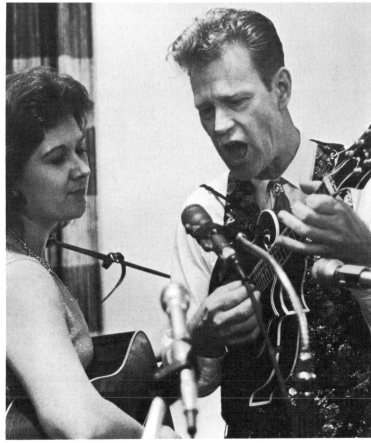

CHORD DICTIONARY

Two different ways of making each of the major, seventh and minor chords are given. In some cases one of the two employs open strings, which means this position would be used where the strings were to be allowed to ring (as on stops or endings, for example). A circle above a string (o) means that string is played open.

The number on the dot indicates which finger is to be used. Where the chord is played up the neck, the fret at which the first string is noted appears at the right.

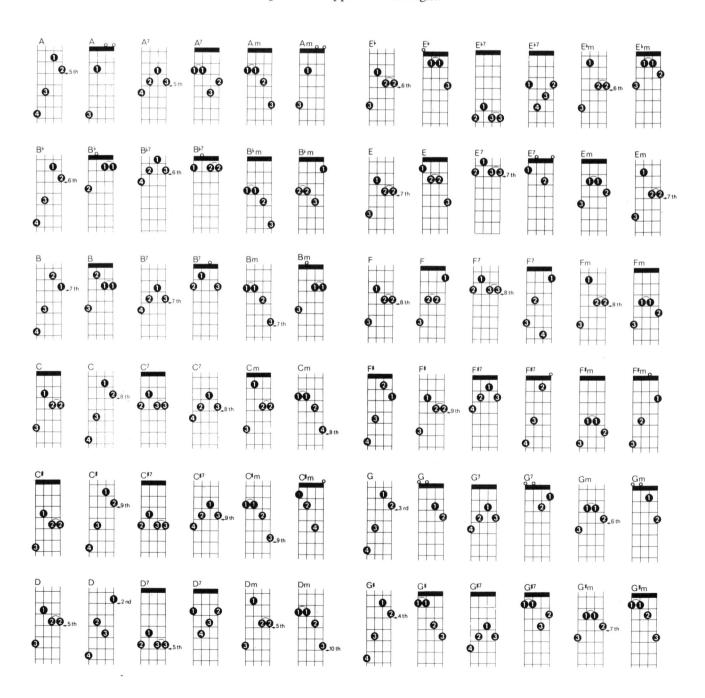